EIGHT
WOMEN
of the
AMERICAN
STAGE

EIGHT
WOMEN
of the
AMERICAN
STAGE

Talking About
Acting

Roy Harris

with

MARY ALICE · JUDITH IVEY · CHERRY JONES
MARY MC DONNELL · DONNA MURPHY
SARAH JESSICA PARKER · GWEN VERDON
JOANNE WOODWARD

Foreword by Emily Mann
McCarter Theatre
Princeton, NJ

HEINEMANN
Portsmouth, NH

Heinemann
A division of Reed Elsevier, Inc.
361 Hanover Street
Portsmouth, NH 03801-3912

Offices and agents throughout the world.

Library of Congress Cataloging-in-Publication Data

Eight women of the American stage : Mary Alice, Judith Ivey, Cherry
    Jones, Mary McDonnell, Donna Murphy, Sarah Jessica Parker, Gwen
    Verdon, Joanne Woodward Talking About Acting / by Roy Harris ; foreword
    by Emily Mann.
        p.   cm.
    ISBN 0-435-07040-1 (alk. paper)
    1. Acting.   2. Actors—United States—Interviews.   3. Actresses—
United States—Interviews.   I. Harris, Roy, 1945–   .
PN2061.E44   1997
792'.028'082—dc21   97-25871
                                                                                        CIP

Editor: Lisa A. Barnett
Production: Renée Le Verrier
Cover design: Darci Mehall
Manufacturing: Louise Richardson

Printed in the United States of America on acid-free paper.

00   99   98   97   DA   1   2   3   4   5   6

Contents

Acknowledgments

ℚ⊗ℚ

Thanks, first, to my many friends who listened to me talk about this book, often ad nauseam—especially my daughter, Miranda, who never *seemed* to tire of the subject. Wendy Wasserstein, a more loyal friend one could not hope for. André Bishop, who allowed me use of Lincoln Center Theater's facilities for interviews, editing, etc., and his incredible staff: Assistant Julia Judge, persona extraordinaire; Mari Eckroate, organizational empress; Daniel Swee (whose casting connections have been, and are, invaluable) and his great associate, Cindy Tolan; Anne Cattaneo, who knows more people than any one person should; Tom Cott; and Anne Tanaka.

And all the others who helped in so many different ways: Joan Marcus, Susan Chicoine, David Milligan, Carol Fishman, Mike Phillips, Jane Harmon, Julie Baldauff, Shelley Bernstein, Alexis Shorter, James FitzSimmons, Donnell B. Stern, Rian Keating, Jim Carnahan, Darice O'Mara, Tony Walton, Stephen Stout, Ron Rifkin, Robbie Baitz, and Joseph Neal; Philip Rinaldi; James Morrison; Adrian Bryan-Bryan, Erin Dunn, and Andy Shearer of Boneau-Bryan-Brown; Carol Ochs of the 52nd Street Project; Kim Powers and Bill O'Donnell of WNET-Channel 13; Reagan Fletcher of the Shubert Archive; Betty Corwin and Patrick Hoffman of the Lincoln Center Library for the Performing Arts; Rob Scott and Dena Consolini of the Museum of Radio and Television; and the costume designers, Jess Goldstein and Martin Pakledinaz.

Foreword

ᗑᗅ

Eight Women of the American Stage is a remarkable read. Eight of our greatest performers reveal in great depth and detail how they work; how they create a role; and in so doing, reveal the secrets of their individual creative processes.

Certainly, there have been many other books and articles containing interviews of actors and actresses, but what makes this book unique is that the interviewer is an insider, a rare breed of stage manager who has spent a lifetime in love with the creative process and the actors who embody its mysteries. Or *actresses*, to be more accurate: Roy Harris confesses in his preface that it is the work of America's greatest stage actresses that inspired him as a child and marked him for a life in the theatre.

Since an actor's work is always done in the privacy of his or her own home and behind the closed doors of a rehearsal room, we don't often have the chance to observe or understand it. Roy Harris' detailed interviews with these eight actresses have given us the unique opportunity to see behind those doors, to hear from the women themselves how they approach the business of performing and rehearsing. They talk on a highly sophisticated level because they are speaking to a fellow professional, an insider; in some cases, the very insider whom they have trusted to be in the room with them when they have done their most intimate and emotionally dangerous work.

I have had the great privilege of working with four of these extraordinary actresses and have admired the work of all of them throughout my career. As a director, I was fascinated to hear them talk about the individual roles they have created, how they craft their roles, and what they need in rehearsal to do their best work. We directors rarely hear this articulated. Not surprisingly, the eight actresses have highly individual methods of working from pre-rehearsal preparation through the closing-night performance. To hear from each of them is a revelation.

This book is a gift to anyone who loves the theatre, but it is essential reading for all of us who make it. Roy Harris invites us inside the rehearsal room, inside the hearts, and inside the minds of eight of our greatest performers. It is a privilege to be allowed inside what Mary McDonnell calls "that mysterious place I go."

Emily Mann
McCarter Theatre
Princeton, NJ

Preface

ᘓᑋᘒ

I don't know the secret. It's a constant search for it.

—Sir Derek Jacobi

When *Conversations in the Wings*, my first book of interviews about acting technique, was published in April 1994 (Heinemann), I assumed I was done with the subject of the whys and wherefores of that great mystery, acting. The thirteen actors and actresses interviewed over a two-and-a-half-year period had answered my questions about how they worked on a role thoughtfully, sincerely, eagerly, and with great good cheer and humor. I had acquired a wealth of information about acting technique from a diverse group of working professionals, all of whom I had great respect for before our interviews, and for whom I had even more as a result of our talking. Through the details of their quite diverse careers and lives, they had solidified my love for a subject that has been variously described as:

—to be the part; to be it in your arms, your legs; to be what you are acting, to be it all over.

—Dion Boucicault

—that natural gift whereby he is enabled to enter into, comprehend and interpret the experiences of many persons, often most unlike himself.

—David Belasco

—the ability whereby a man who, through the medium of his own body, imitates the manners and passions of other men.

—William Archer

This rather eclectic assortment of definitions—from an actor/playwright, an actor/manager/playwright, and a critic—covers more than a century of thought on the subject and illustrates the essence of acting: one person becomes another.

Several months after the book's publication, something happened that made me realize the subject was hardly closed. I got a note from Joanne Woodward, with whom I had worked twice as a stage manager. Thanking me for sending her a copy of the book, she wrote: "I'd love to be included in the next edition." That one sentence was all I needed to spur my energy and imagination a second time. The chance to talk with Joanne, one of America's great actors, about her technique made me realize the subject described by Dion Boucicault as "to be what you are acting, to be it all over" is, for me, still endlessly fascinating and magical. I'm not sure that enough can ever be said about it, because the place in the self where a performance begins is so mysterious. Perhaps that is why, in an interview in the *London Times*, Sir Derek Jacobi said about acting: "I don't know the secret. It's a constant search for it."

I have loved theatre and acting for as long as I can remember, though I certainly didn't see either as a subject of knowledge or education. Seeing theatre and watching actors at work simply made for great pleasure. My strongest feelings about acting were mostly the result, like millions of other Americans, of exposure to that remarkable phenomenon: the movies. And I loved them. I have vivid memories of many film performances—and for some reason, the most vivid of these are women: Anna Magnani's lusty agitation as she throws Burt Lancaster out of her house in *The Rose Tattoo*, Deborah Kerr's reticence as she tries to tell David Niven that she loves him in *Separate Tables*, Shirley MacLaine's hesitant explanation to Jack Lemmon for why she tried to take her life in *The Apartment*, Susan Hayward's gutsy defiance as she faced death in *I Want to Live!*, and Marilyn Monroe, draped in what appeared to be a gossamer gown of black bugle beads, exuding a remarkable combination of innocence and sensuality as she sang "I Wanna Be Loved by You" to Tony Curtis who was playing the saxophone, in drag, in Billy Wilder's *Some Like It Hot*.

I had no idea then that I was watching some incredible displays of acting technique. (That realization came much later when I found out how much work—no matter how pleasurable it may be—goes into making that "magic" happen.) Those movies just seemed like heaven to me. And they made me want to be an actor myself. So, like thousands of other young people across America, I took part in community theatre; in college, at the University of Alabama, I majored in Theatre and English, acting in as many shows as possible; and during the summers, I did seasons of stock in "package" houses like the Ivoryton Playhouse in Connecticut, among others. After graduation, I moved to New York to study acting at the American Academy of Dramatic Arts, where I took courses in basic acting technique, voice and diction, acting styles, ballet, movement for actors, singing, make-up, mime, etc. I saw almost every show that opened on Broadway in the 1967–1968 season. Reduced-priced preview tickets were made available to us through the Academy for many shows, and if not, I bought standing room for $1.50. That year—which William Goldman has described with such vigorous detail in his "candid look at Broadway" called *The Season*—really confirmed my great love for live theatre. I saw Zoe Caldwell in *The Prime of Miss Jean Brodie*; Arthur Hill, Colleen Dewhurst, and Ingrid Bergman in O'Neill's *More Stately Mansions*; Maureen Stapleton and George C. Scott in *Plaza Suite*; Albert Finney and Zena Walker in *Joe Egg*; Marian Seldes in *Before You Go*; Eileen Atkins in *The Promise*; Ruth White and Henderson Forsythe in Pinter's *The Birthday Party*; Rosemary Harris, Clayton Corzatte, Eva Le Gallienne, and other members of the APA Repertory Company in *Pantagleize*, *Exit the King*, and *You Can't Take It with You*; and many, many more. There was no show I didn't want to see, and very few I missed.

How Much We Can Learn About Acting

Within a year of leaving the Academy, I had had several rather good experiences as an actor, though I always had a nagging feeling that something just wasn't right. After several years of what I think I already knew unconsciously were fairly lifeless performances, I realized that my abilities in theatre lay in another direction. My penchant for neatness, organization, and giving orders (however well they may be disguised) made me much more suitable as a stage manager.

I have never regretted that choice, first, because it was right for me, second and almost as important, because being in rehearsals made it possible for me to observe other actors working. In actuality, becoming a stage manager made my real love for acting become clear to me. I could observe with a friendly, uncompetitive eye how other actors work, and that's just what I've done for nearly twenty years. Somehow, for me, an understanding of *how* to create a living, breathing character on stage was more important than an ability to *do* it.

Considering the best way to approach the interviews for this book, I came to feel that if I looked at acting technique over an entire career, it would give both a new and added dimension to the subject and make clear how much these actors have to teach us about acting. For instance, has the way of working altered or changed in any way? In her interview, Mary McDonnell explains that she no longer needs to do certain kinds of pre-rehearsal work on a character because she's more sure of herself now than when she began her professional career in 1978. "When I first started out," she says, "I used to break it down very specifically, because I was afraid not to have all these things answered. I try now to leave it as mysterious as possible."

Another area for discussion: What has been learned over the years about technique itself? Responding to a question about why she'd been afraid of studying voice earlier in her career, Donna Murphy relates this: "I was unsure of being technical about something that I had always been instinctive about. I didn't want to approach songs from a place of sound, even though I was certainly aware of sound. . . . A certain part of me is regretful that I didn't have the technique earlier on, but then I think that I wouldn't have other things that I now have."

Other questions at the heart of these interviews that enhance our knowledge of acting as a subject: What has changed in the way of working? How important is technique in the longevity of a career? After a rich and rather humorous discussion of her Academy Award–winning performance in *The Three Faces of Eve*, I asked Joanne Woodward if she had the chance to do the part again, would she do anything differently? Her answer is straightforward, yet very telling: "I would do Jane differently," and she explains in outline what she means. The fact that after nearly forty years she would change one of the aspects of Eve is a sign of the true artist and, for me, a sign of why her work continues to grow in depth, grace, and assurance: She never stops learning.

Enlarging the Scope of What We Can Learn

The questions that I asked in the course of these interviews are, as a whole, similar to those asked in *Conversations in the Wings*. They are a learning aid whose purpose is to accomplish two things: first, to act as an outline, so there's some authentic way to compare one actor's way of working with another's; and second, to cover the acting process from pre-rehearsal work through the performance itself.

I found, however, after the first couple of these interviews that the form needed to be "looser" this time. It's my belief that *Conversations in the Wings* showed, arguably more or less, that there is something called acting technique among American actors. While hopefully reiterating that, the interviews in this book allow for more variety and diversity, therefore enlarging the scope of what we can learn. And they are consciously less structured. For instance, I didn't see the necessity to ask *everyone* interviewed about the differences between acting on stage and acting for the camera. Where the details of a career impelled a question, it was asked; if they didn't, it wasn't.

The interviews themselves took place over a period of eighteen months. While researching, organizing, and conducting them, I was also stage-managing A.R. Gurney's *Sylvia* at the Manhattan Theatre Club, Jon Robin Baitz's *A Fair Country* at Lincoln Center Theater, and Tennessee Williams' *Summer and Smoke* at the Roundabout Theatre Company— three experiences that greatly helped form this book. The first interview, with Joanne Woodward, took place on May 25, 1995, and the final one, with Mary McDonnell, on October 10, 1996. They were each about two-and-a-half hours long and were transcribed verbatim shortly after the interview. I took at least a month—in some cases, several—to read, re-read, and re-read again each interview so I could understand as clearly as possible the dramatic shape of each woman's knowledge.

In the editing process, I discovered that the voice of the interviewer (my own) lessened the potency of what each actress said about her work, life, and career. So for the published version, I decided to lose the "interview" format and edit each actress' observations into a kind of informal "essay." As I worked on these changes, I was amazed to see what a large difference it made: My implicit presence made the knowledge in each interview more explicit and dramatic. The focus appeared to be in the right place.

Why Only Women?

Why only women? This is a question I've been asked (with varying degrees of agitation and calm, usually depending on the gender of the questioner) rather often as I've worked on these interviews. There are essentially two answers.

First: The world has come pretty far in the way it sees the place of women in our lives and culture. (One instance significant to the subject of this book: In Greek theatre, there were no "actresses." Men played all the roles, as they did for nearly two thousand more years. Now, however, according to Actors' Equity Association, women comprise forty-seven percent of its membership.) With all the changes in how women are seen—and it certainly goes far beyond the present subject—the world hasn't come far enough. Interviewing a number of women, it seemed to me, about how they saw their own technique and its applications, would, hopefully, add to the world's respect for the infinite and rich possibilities of the minds of women.

Second: As I thought about what should be included in this book, there were a number of images that didn't, and wouldn't, go away: Anna Magnani, Deborah Kerr, Shirley MacLaine, Susan Hayward, Marilyn Monroe. Those great women of the silver screen, whose film appearances in the 1950s first made me care for acting and theatre, kept returning. In ways they likely could never have guessed, these five women, among a dozen or so others (one of whom is in this book), have been an inspiration towards my love and respect for and undertanding of the "magic" of acting.

A Romance of a Very Unique Kind

I think it can easily be said that over a number of years I've had a romance of a very unique kind with each of the eight women interviewed in these pages. Four of them close-up from rehearsal and performance scrutiny: Judith Ivey, Mary McDonnell, Sarah Jessica Parker, and Joanne Woodward. The other four from an admiring distance: Mary Alice, Cherry Jones, Donna Murphy, and Gwen Verdon.

The first, and most distant: I fell in love with Gwen Verdon's photograph as Lola in *Damn Yankees* when it appeared on the cover of *Time*, a magazine my father read religiously all through my growing-up years. To this ten-year-old, she was the epitome of what a glamorous musical star should be: bright, beautiful, with a voluptuous physiognomy. At that time, Broadway stars were national figures (alas, because of the all-consuming presence of television these days, that's no longer true). Though I did see her recreate Lola in the film version, it was to be ten years before I saw Ms. Verdon live. Her performance in *Sweet Charity* will forever stand, in my mind, for what a great musical comedy performance should be: both over-the-top and grounded in reality, both funny and deeply touching, and with emotions so strong that the characters are impelled to sing and dance them.

Gwen Verdon had a Broadway musical comedy career that spanned three full decades. The year after she stopped performing musically, 1979, Donna Murphy got her first Equity job, as a back-up singer in *They're Playing Our Song*. Ms. Murphy is now one of the few bonafide Broadway musical stars of the '90s. A premier interpreter of contemporary musical composers, notably as Fosca in Stephen Sondheim's *Passion*, in 1996 she showed she was equally at home with more standard musical fare. She brought a serious, intelligent intimacy to Mrs. Anna in the revival of Rodgers and Hammerstein's *The King and I* (still playing to capacity houses at the time of this writing).

Ms. Murphy shares a remarkable ability with Cherry Jones and Mary Alice: all three bring a luminous reality to everything they do on stage.

In 1995, Ms. Jones completely won over audiences with her heart-breaking performance as Catherine Sloper in *The Heiress* (a performance that rightly won her all the major acting awards that season, including the Tony Award). While allowing us to see a reticent, insecure young woman living in the shadow of her long-dead mother, Cherry Jones revealed, often through silence, a self buried so deeply within Catherine that she herself didn't know it was there.

Mary Alice happens to be one of the great African-American actresses of the twentieth century. What makes her great is her ability to take us into the naked emotional territory of the mind and have us feel those emotions as strongly as the character does. That I can now say I know these four women, at least to a degree, through their interviews is a source of pride.

I have known, over a number of years and in varying degrees, the remaining four women in this book from professional relationships. I was in the room as each created a great, multi-layered, much-applauded performance, one that stirred audiences with its intense emotional reality. This fact is not only a source of pride, but, as you'll see, quite literally, one of the sources of this book.

I was there when Mary McDonnell created her Alma Winemiller and completely reinvented our notion of who this Tennessee Williams heroine is (a reinvention not entirely welcomed by some). We knew that this woman whom Williams brought to life in *Summer and Smoke* was a major figure in American drama, but we had no idea to what extent she is a woman of our own time. Mary McDonnell showed us.

I observed Judith Ivey create her wrenching performance as the angry, troubled Patrice Burgess in Jon Robin Baitz's *A Fair Country*, runner-up for the 1996 Pulitzer Prize for Drama. She took us on a journey that was truly an experience in our understanding the wounded humanity of all people.

Sarah Jessica Parker completely changed all my previous ideas about how far an actor can go on stage and still create a firm, believable reality, in her hilarious, and ultimately touching, performance as the street-smart pooch in A.R. Gurney's *Sylvia*.

Joanne Woodward, whose work I was becoming acquainted with about the same time I saw Gwen Verdon's photograph on the cover of *Time*, has been a major part of my love of theatre and acting—perhaps more so than any other single performer. A fellow Southerner (a trait shared with Mary Alice and Cherry Jones), she came to New York in the early '50s and, first through the media of live television and theatre and then later the movies, proceeded to make an indelible mark on

American culture. I had one of the most exciting stage managing experiences of my career watching Joanne create and play Alexandra del Lago in Williams' *Sweet Bird of Youth*. She brought her own unique, instinctive reality to the role that she had seen Geraldine Page create some thirty years earlier opposite her husband, Paul Newman.

Had I not taken part in the four women's journeys to these characters, I might not have been impelled to do this book at all. I will forever be grateful to them, and to the other four women here, for stirring me so deeply in the first place and for their generosity in allowing me to be a part of their individual work processes. They are indeed great women of the American stage.

"I don't work from any conscious physicality. With The Heiress, *I thought about my hands, and I knew any extra fluttering was certainly not Catherine."*

as Catherine Sloper in *The Heiress*

Cherry Jones
Emotion Within Stillness

In the fall of 1990, a friend from Boston called. "I just saw a great production of *Twelfth Night* at the American Repertory Theatre," she said with abundant, and for her, uncommon energy. "You have to see it." A week later, I took the train to Cambridge and saw the production. It was good—colorful, energetic, bright, and with a vitality and elan I think Shakespeare himself would have liked.

But the astounding thing about the production was the Viola of Cherry Jones, an actress whose work I was unfamiliar with until that performance. Golden curls bobbling around her rosy cheeks, this Viola had an energetic grace, a bold assertive intelligence that I'd never seen before. When Viola (pretending to be Cesario) said to Olivia:

Make me a willow cabin at your gate,
And call upon my soul within the house,

I heard something completely new in terms of the meaning of love. This woman-pretending-to-be-a-man-pretending-to-love-a-woman says further to Olivia:

Write loyal canons of contemned love
And sing them loud even in the dead of night;
Halloo your name to the reverberate hills,

I

And make the babbling gossip of the air
Cry out "Olivia!"

I saw that Viola was falling in love with Olivia with the same depth, sincerity, and force she does later with Orsino, and I understood more clearly why Shakespeare wrote those "britches" roles. My perception of love and what it can, and indeed may be, was altered forever.

A year or so later, in the Broadway production of Timberlake Wertenbaker's *Our Country's Good*, Cherry played Liz Mordern, a convict in a penal colony in Australia. Angry, vengeful, filthy, foul language spewing constantly—she couldn't have been more different from Viola—Liz let forth with a fury I'll never forget. Yet, simultaneously, we felt another life hidden inside this wrathful, furious woman, and it made our empathy for her unusually deep.

One of Cherry Jones' many abilities as an actress is to unearth what the Victorian poet Matthew Arnold called "The Buried Life." As the disguised Olivia, she might be wonderfully energetic and outgoing. We always get, though, more than a glimpse of the welter of feeling inside. On the other hand, she might seem quiet, thoughtful, composed, as either Catherine Sloper in *The Heiress* or Hannah Jelkes in *The Night of the Iguana* (which at the time of our interview had just opened on Broadway). No matter how serene she might seem, still we begin to fathom, as Arnold says, "the mystery of this heart which beats/ So wild, so deep in us."

I truly can't remember a time—yes, I'm one of those—when I didn't want to be an actress. When I was a little girl, I was in a dance recital. I loved the interaction with the audience and the laughter and applause. Also, I was in a creative dramatics course from about the age of six. Every Wednesday afternoon after school we'd get on a little platform stage, and Miss Ruby Crider would turn us into shoelaces and birds in trees and the wind blowing over mountaintops.

I'm from a small southern town—Paris, Tennessee—and I didn't get to see much theatre. My earliest feelings about acting came from films. I remember, as a thirteen-year-old, seeing Maureen Stapleton in *Airport*. That performance had a profound effect on me. I also saw great films like *To Kill a Mockingbird* and, almost as much as the acting, I was touched by stories that really affected the way you approached life.

I did get to the Barter Theatre in Virginia when I was quite young, maybe eleven or so, and saw *The Country Girl*. At the end of the play the actress said these beautiful, final poetic lines. The lights went down on her face, and I was aware of the "ghosting" of the light. Not knowing it was a technical thing, I thought it was her soul sending up a final spark. I remember thinking it was the most remarkable sight, a miracle happening before my eyes.

This may sound strange but because I'm not a thinker, or an intellect, when I feel I *have* to do a particular role, I start to feel the muscularity of the character. Of course, the worthiness of the entire play is important to me too. But I start to feel the tension in their bones, the way they hold themselves, whether their breathing is deep or shallow, how they move. Through the writing, I start to feel them physically. Somehow feeling them physically leads me directly to their soul. It's an outward reaction to whatever it is that's fueling them.

The roles I've felt most successful in have made for that response almost immediately upon reading the script. I certainly felt it with Liz Mordern in *Our Country's Good*. The director, Mark Lamos, was quick to push me in an extreme direction with that character. Once I realized I could go that far with her, I felt a tremendous release. I had a similar, very strong response to Catherine Sloper in *The Heiress*. Now, with Paula Vogel's play, *The Baltimore Waltz*, at Circle Rep, I had no idea what the play was about. And I said "yes" before I even read it. In the past I often accepted a role that way—I depended on the kindness of artistic directors. Now that I'm in a slightly different jockeying position, I don't know if I'll approach things as I did. I hope I will because I've had such luck with it for the past fifteen years.

I've had a long-lasting relationship, and still do, with the American Repertory Theatre in Cambridge. That was like being in the army. You basically went where they sent you. It was a wonderful way to train because they sometimes sent you in directions you never thought you could pull off—and sometimes I could and sometimes I couldn't.

Rehearsals, and Before

Once I've decided to do a role, before rehearsals start, I do very little conscious work. Actually, there've been a couple of productions where I've read the play only once before going into rehearsals. I believe it really has to be the chemistry within the rehearsal room, and you want to save yourself in a way. It's like knowing you're about to meet a lover. But you don't know who they are or what they look like. You can get very excited knowing it's about to happen and knowing you're going to fall deeply in love—whether it lasts is another matter. I approach upcoming rehearsals with the idea of a great impending affair.

I don't know exactly what I'm looking for from other actors in rehearsal. I think it's whatever they truly have to give; also, professional behavior and hopefully a light heart. Every once in a blue moon, you'll run across someone who has some very strong, preconceived notion of how something should be. If the director can't successfully make the actor yield to his own vision, then you've got to figure out how you're going to fit in with both views. I have fond memories, though, of almost every actor I've ever been on stage with. I haven't run into any who've made my flesh crawl. I was fortunate to work with a company of actors at the American Repertory Theatre all those years. We knew each other so well, we were like a great NBA team. We would pass that ball and know that we were never going to be left out on our own and let down.

I remember we were doing Serban's production of *The Three Sisters*, and it was so successful that they decided to bring it back a few more times over the course of several months, but really just scattered throughout the rep season. Cheryl Giannini said, "It's so poignant doing Chekhov once a month." Now we could never have done that had we not been working together constantly in all the other shows.

I can say what I like in a director in the rehearsal process, but it doesn't necessarily mean what I come to love later. Ideally, I like someone who's completely obsessed, possessed, and committed 150 percent: Directors who are so excited about the text and spend almost every moment in the rehearsal room exploring it. Andrei Serban was a big influence on me, and I can promise you there was not a moment lost or wasted in his rehearsals. There's almost a frenzy in his rehearsals because your adrenaline is coming out of the top of your head.

Approaching the Role

I don't work from any conscious physicality. It mostly just happens. It was interesting with *The Heiress*. I thought about my hands, and I knew any extra fluttering would be flamboyant—that was certainly not Catherine. So I had to figure out something interesting that would contain her—something exciting to watch and yet self-conscious. There was a kind of hand movement that I used with Hannah Jelkes in the original Goodman production of *Night of the Iguana*. I stole a little bit for Catherine, especially the hand across the waist. When I first approached Hannah in Chicago in 1994—two years ago—I was so caught up in the stylization of the character as described by Tennessee. He has that remarkable description when she enters. I've never been given a stage direction like this:

Hannah is remarkable-looking—ethereal, almost ghostly. She suggests a Gothic cathedral image of a medieval saint, but animated.

She could be thirty, she could be forty: she is totally feminine and yet androgynous-looking—almost timeless.

Beautiful. He gives you this incredible shape. It's a springboard into understanding what her function in the play is.

So I stole a little bit of Hannah for Catherine a year later. Now, coming back into playing Hannah after having played Catherine, I thought, "Well, I can't just keep doing that same gesture." Actually, I'm still uncomfortable with that part of Hannah because I pinched a little too much for Catherine, never dreaming that I would be doing these ladies back-to-back-to-back. It's something I'm still working on, along with much about the character herself.

I've realized recently I'm not sure I'm really ready to play Hannah yet. There's a reason the actresses who usually play this role are in their forties and even their fifties. There's a kind of maturity and enlightenment in this remarkable woman that younger actresses don't easily have. You can fake *down*, but it's hard to fake *up*, especially when you're dealing with such a soulful, spiritual person. When Bob Falls, artistic director of the Goodman, asked me to play Hannah originally, I read the play and was very uncertain. I thought, "Good grief, how do you do this play?" Stylistically it's all over the place, and I don't think there have ever been any definitive productions of it in this country. It's such a magnificent play, and more than any other play I've done, everybody has an opinion about how it should be done. Everybody's got an opinion about Chekhov too, but he's done so frequently that they deal with the fact that each generation is going to have a different approach. But with *Iguana*, people are fierce in their opinions.

Overall, it's been rewarding to play. But I'm afraid I got spoiled with a year of total bliss on *The Heiress*, where everybody and his Uncle Joe seemed to respond to it positively. We're in the "dog days" right now because we've been battered around by the press *and* by our friends. We're at that delicate stage where we've lost some confidence in ourselves and the production. I think what's going to happen is that we're going to bottom out completely, give a couple of dreadful shows, and then build up again. I am confident it'll recharge itself.

The Rehearsal Process

Once rehearsals begin, the first thing I do is make sure I know all my lines. I'm a real one-track horse. I can't do two things at once: looking at a page is one thing and trying to get the play on its feet is another. So I always try to get my lines down cold, but learn them in as neutral a way as possible.

Also, by the third or fourth rehearsal, you have an idea of at least the silhouette of the costume. The minute I get up on my feet, I always work with rehearsal clothes. That way I can start to imagine what it's going to be like to move in "this outfit." But mainly my homework is to learn the lines and to be alert, fresh, and in a good mood.

I've come to feel that you approach every role differently. I think I have a different technique with every role. But I've never been able to analyze. Sometimes an intention will come to me in performance. I'll suddenly go, "Ooooh, I see what that's about." And some directors will lead you in that direction. But if it's really working, you don't need to talk about it. I would say that I'm basically an instinctive actress, but I wish in a way I were more analytical. Look at Eileen Atkins, whom I adore. There's a woman who is brilliant and an intellect and has a most amazing facility for the language. She's got every tool, and she possesses a beautiful soul. Instinct is wonderful but to have the kind of tools that an Eileen Atkins or a Maggie Smith has—well, it means the sky's the limit. I would like to be able to reach a little higher in that direction. I don't think I have the mind of an artist. I do think I have an artist's soul but not the mind.

Sometimes actors do have too much "technique," with quotes. You see certain actresses—and I probably look at actresses more critically because I am one—and sometimes the older they get, the more mannered and controlled the work becomes. You've got this bag of tricks to pull from, and you're distracted because you're moving into a part of life where parents are ill—or friends—or there are children who are screwed up—and you get tired. And I have great compassion for people whose work becomes tired. It becomes uninvested. I'm not sure how you avoid that as an actor. I suppose, stay curious and have an active imagination.

Costumes

I'm tremendously affected by the clothes I'm going to wear. Often I leave it up to the designer, but once in a while I'll get a flash of something prior to rehearsals. I remember I played the mother in the premiere of Chris Durang's *Baby with the Bathwater*—a very bizarre character. I got a flash of her in the Jackie Kennedy salmon Dallas suit, and a plastic headband with pouffy hair and sunglasses, a double tumbler of bourbon, and a Vassar '49 take on the world. Once I got that, everything else fell into place. Mark Linn-Baker directed. Tony Shalhoub, Karen MacDonald, Marianne Owen—we had a blast.

In 1993, I did *The Good Person of Szechwan* in Chicago for Frank Galati. Susan Hilferty (who also did the costumes for *Iguana*) brought in a design for Shui Ta, the evil other half of Shen Teh, the good person of Szechwan. Her idea was that he was street tough, initially. And as his business grew, his clothes would change. But I felt that because the production was one of those cross-cultural, cross-time concepts, from the beginning he should enter with utter, terrifying, intimidating authority. I saw him as sort of a John D. Rockefeller, turn-of-the-century, steel baron/railroad baron, high starched collar, an ascot and a mustache—very imposing, so that no one would ever dare question his authority. Susan immediately liked the idea.

That was one of the few times I actually played in my closet before rehearsals. I found some kind of blazer and an ascot and a man's collar, and I got some burnt cork—and took it with me to Chicago. I started playing around, and I thought, "Oh, this is fun." It made me feel good and it made me feel powerful. Now it screwed me up a bit in rehearsal because I had thought of Shui Ta more as her evil, protective great uncle. So he was very stiff, more your capitalist banker type. But it wasn't working. I knew something had to change because it wasn't fun to play. One night my girlfriend Mary was in Chicago, and we were talking. "It's not there," I said. "It's stiff and boring." At some point in our talk, it came to me: "He really should be her twin. He's not old. He's young. So he can also be sexy." When I started thinking of him as her twin, as opposed to her protective uncle, I immediately found the sexiness of the man, which needed to be there. They were more like equals, which made it more interesting dynamically and truer to what Brecht was saying.

The way clothes affect an actor, and are an integral part of how he sees the role, is fascinating. When we were working on *The Heiress*, Jane Greenwood, who designed the clothes, was so thoughtful about how I saw myself and myself-as-Catherine. She was so dear with me. There's a funny little story: I went to a fitting early on because we had to do the mock-up for the photograph that James McMullan was going to use for the poster. I was sitting there with Jane and her assistant, Ilona, and we were looking through these wonderful period books and old photographs. The froufrou on these dresses was making me very nervous. So I said, "Well, that first dress should be completely inappropriate, but it shouldn't be irritating." Ilona was so shocked. She looked at me and said, "Jane Greenwood could never design anything that was irritating." She was so protective.

But it was always that way with me—bows and ribbons just didn't work. My grandmother loved to sew. She used to dress my younger sister and me within an inch of our lives. My sister was all peaches and cream—she got all the lace and bows. And I was so tailored, I was practically in West Point clothes.

Jane had originally designed all sorts of things over the bodice of the white dress Catherine wears at the end of the play. It was all bows and flowers and fluffy things, and I felt so uncomfortable. She took one look at me and started ripping off the bows and flowers. She said, "We just can't dress you up, can we? It must be very simple, mustn't it?" The great thing for me about that white costume, which is the last thing we see her in, is its simplicity. There's a kind of freedom in it; we see more of her than anywhere else in the play. Its openness is such a contrast to the other clothes she wears.

I once had an interesting experience with a costume—actually, it was more the wig. I played Viola in a production of *Twelfth Night*, directed by Andrei Serban at ART. In rehearsal, I worked in my own hair, and it was short, straight, and brown. Andrei wanted Viola and Sebastian to not only look alike but to be like cherubim with these golden locks. Now when I put on that blonde wig, I was horrified. I felt like Goldie Hawn circa 1968. "This is just awful," I thought, "I look like a French poodle." I couldn't stand it. The show itself was terribly theatrical, as Andrei's productions usually are. After wearing it a bit, I came to feel that it gave everything I did a heightened quality, and it helped me get to heightened emotions internally. Eventually, I saw that it made a big difference in how I felt.

I often have a feeling about how the hair should look. In *The Night of the Iguana*, Williams describes Hannah as blonde. The idea to make my Hannah's hair darker and silver-streaked was really from Susan Hilferty and Bob Falls. I think the decision to go with gray was the idea of a trilogy with Rev. Shannon and my grandfather Nonno. Billy Petersen, who plays Shannon, is prematurely gray, and then Nonno, of course, is silver-gray. The gray would also give me some age. We first did the play two years ago, and I can sometimes look younger than I am. I think they wanted to age me up a bit.

The Audience: "You Hear Them Listening"

When I first get an audience, I fight them. I realized recently that a pattern has developed. And I don't know why really because I like audiences. But the first time in front of an audience—with both *The Heiress* and *Iguana*—I gave one of the worst performances ever. I didn't want to be there. And that never happened to me in the past. I'm a good old workhorse. Put on my harness, and I go to work.

I realized it's a sadness to me to give it over to the audience. I love the rehearsal room and the camaraderie there. That's when the cast falls in love with each other. Once you get in performance, you see each other three hours in the evening. When that audience shows up, I

Cherry Jones with William Petersen as Reverend Shannon in The Night of the Iguana.

mourn the loss of all that. But then I go on from there and embrace the next stage. You learn from an audience when you're being most truthful—and when you're worthy of being listened to. Because you hear them listening, or not listening.

Playing *The Heiress* was very satisfying to do nightly because of the effect it had on people. It's such a simple story, but the way that it would touch people was amazing. Literate, well-educated men and women would leave the theatre in these heated debates over the fate of Catherine Sloper: Had she done the right thing? That is so rare in any form of entertainment—to get people that involved.

And the kids would come to see it. So many times it would be inner-city kids. And you'd think, they're going to look at these old, ugly, white people in these odd costumes. What the hell are they going to think? And you know what? They would just lose their minds, because ultimately it's a father-daughter play, a parent-child story, and they would just go bananas. They were so excited by it that it was like a rock concert at the end.

Acting Problems in a Long Run

The longest run I've ever done was *The Heiress*. Being in a long run presents acting problems that being in a show for only thirty performances doesn't. When my first father and lover—Philip Bosco and Jon Tenney—left the show, Donald Moffatt and Michael Cumpsty came on. It was wonderful because their very presence gave us all new life. It was a completely different play. Any boredom that might have set in was alleviated.

Those of us who had been doing it for several months had gotten a bit tired. I found I had a desire to "deepen my interpretation of the role," and the result was it had become a bit grand. It was a little Edwardian. Gerry Gutierrez came back, took one look at it, rapped my knuckles, and I "took out the improvements." I don't think my "improvements" had to do with winning the Tony Award. I sincerely felt I was bringing new and deeper and richer colors to the role. The lesson I learned: I was making it more baroque. And I couldn't see it; I was blind to it. So that discovery was very important. I don't think I erred in that direction again for the seven months we played.

Another acting problem in a long run: You can only cry over a particular situation for so long, and then you've mourned and you have to move on. What I found fascinating in playing Catherine was, I was able to use little personal emotional buttons to get myself where I needed to be. I found I could hook into a scene through a kind of tremulous emotionality that I had concocted offstage in the wings or on stage while others were talking. With Catherine it was fairly easy because she didn't say a lot. I could be sitting there imagining all sorts of horrible personal dilemmas and then say something every few minutes. I realized that my mind as an older actress is starting to do a wonderful thing where I can literally be using something from my own life to fuel me and crosswire it with the situation I'm playing. I think when I was younger those two parts of my mind stayed very far apart. But there is a danger with this little technique. It can make the character more like you unless you're really careful how you use it.

That's dangerous because that's not where I started in rehearsal in February 1995 with Gerry Gutierrez. Making the character too close to you is as dangerous as becoming baroque or just dull. So you really have to monitor those pitfalls.

There are things in the play so satisfying to anyone watching it. For instance, when Catherine finally tells him off. This is when she's trying to get him to dictate the will. She says:

You want to think of me sitting in dignity in this handsome house, rich, respected, and unloved forever. That is what you think I deserve. But I may fool you, Father. I may take your money and chase after Morris, and squander it all on him. . . . Which do you think I will do?
Dr. Sloper: I don't know.
Catherine: Well, you must decide, and act accordingly.
Dr. Sloper: I can't. I don't know!
Catherine: Perhaps you will in time.
Dr. Sloper: No, I shan't, for I shall be dead.
Catherine: That's right, Father. You'll never know, will you?

Then she helps him up the stairs. You could tell from the audience response it was satisfying for them. But I never really got that telling-off scene the way I wanted. There were a few nights when it exploded in a daring and fresh way. It was very rare, though, that it felt particularly rewarding. I just never felt I nailed it.

You know, in a long run, things change. I remember when we first started, once I got past the scene where Morris abandons her and she breaks down, I'd always consider the rest of the play kind of easy, because she's finally in charge. The release of the tension was always so great that I was relieved to get there.

I had three fathers and three lovers during the run, and the performance changed completely with all three of those men—much more through the father's influence than the lover's, because I was his child and he had formed my life. With each father I had to rethink who I was. They were so different. I realized that it changed how the audience perceived the ending. At the end of the play, I become him. So their response depended on who "him" was.

I honestly think that because you understood the psychology of Donald Moffat (that's one of his great fortes as an actor), the audience was more hopeful about Catherine at the end of the play. She might have a rewarding and giving life because he had been such an extraordinary man. Remak Ramsey's forte with the role was the aristocracy, the arrogance that goes with that; and therefore, I think they were less hopeful about her—perhaps the horizon would not be quite as bright. He was a more rigid and selfish Dr. Sloper, more like Philip. Donald was more egalitarian.

"Broken Gates": Performing Night of the Iguana
The third act of *The Night of the Iguana* is amazing to perform. To be able to say those words every night—even in these days when the

confidence is not completely there—is thrilling. I'm sure you know that most of the great speeches there—the speech about the house of the dying in Shanghai and the "Do you know what a home is?" speech, and that great, great speech that begins—

I still say that I'm not a bird, Mr. Shannon, I'm a human being, and when a member of that fantastic species builds a nest in the heart of another, the question of permanence isn't the first or even the last thing considered . . . necessarily? . . . always?

—those speeches were all cut in the original 1962 Broadway production because Bette Davis did not want the role of Hannah to overshadow her role as Maxine. I can't imagine why Tennessee, with his reputation at that point, would acquiesce to that demand. But perhaps he had grown up with so much conflict all around him he would do anything to avoid it.

I try to keep him close to my heart in that third act. I mean, literally, sometimes when Grandfather is saying that poem, I'm just thanking Tennessee for giving it to us. I think of Tennessee as Nonno sometimes, almost. And when the iguana is being cut loose, I think of his sister Rose finally being allowed to go home to Tom. A woman who has been at the end of her rope since her youth. She's now ancient. She was older than Tennessee, so she'd be close to ninety now.

There are so many great things in the play, especially in the third act. There's this exchange between Hannah and Shannon:

Shannon: What is my problem, Miss Jelkes?
Hannah: The oldest one in the world—the need to believe in something or in someone—almost anyone—almost anything . . . something.
Shannon: Your voice sounds hopeless about it.
Hannah: No, I'm not hopeless about it. In fact, I've discovered something to believe in.
Shannon: Something like . . . God?
Hannah: No.
Shannon: What?
Hannah: Broken gates between people so they can reach each other, even if it's just for one night only.

I got an interesting note at the Roundabout from a woman who wanted me to come to some church and find God. I don't know if she sent it to me because I'm a lesbian or because she'd seen *Iguana* and thought I needed to find God, because, as Hannah, I do say it's not "God," but "broken gates between people." That's always been my religion, and I share it with Tennessee. I've never found faith off this planet, and I have no idea whether there is or there isn't or what's out there. All I know is what I see around us, and it's each other. Tennessee wrote about that better than anyone—the need that makes for "broken gates."

When I first did the play in Chicago two years ago, I was too young emotionally and in terms of life experience to play this role. I said that line in the third act—"Nothing human disgusts me unless it's unkind, violent"—like Greer Garson at her most noble. I realized later that it had to be completely underplayed because it is so important. When you're speaking lines that should be written down and lived by all of us, it's a great responsibility. I was scared to death of this role when I first took it on. I thought, I can't—I'm so unsure now. I was coming out of a difficult time and didn't feel sure about many things.

Directors, in Rehearsal and Previews
Bob Falls is not an actor's director. His approach is about the whole production. He blocks, and you get where he's headed by his blocking. And he gives amazing blocking—like my carrying Nonno on stage. What more do I have to do? It was a little like coming down the stairs in *The Heiress*. You get an entrance like that and all you have to do is show up for the rest of the night. That's how Bob lets you know where he's headed—his blocking.

Gerry Gutierrez is different. He has this omnipotent overview of the world of the play: where it is, where it needs to go, and how it's going to get there. There's this clock ticking in him, and he knows exactly *where* we should be and *when* we should be there. Because the blocking was not the difficult thing about *The Heiress*, Gerry's work really began when we got into previews. And then he was like a laser.

He let us know immediately when it was becoming indulgent, when it was heading in the wrong direction. We used to call his notes "The Gerry Show." He was hysterically funny. He could say the most horrible things to you, and you'd just die laughing. I remember Frances (Sternhagen, who was playing Aunt Penniman) and I were scolded for the way we did the initial story about the veal before Father comes in. He compared what we did to Illinois State Fair pavilion acting. And we knew exactly what he meant.

There's something about Gerry that causes you to trust him implicitly. There may be moments where you disagree with him—our tastes differ. But you know as an actor you can trust him. He'll tell you,

"There is no net here. Either you hit it or look forward to hitting it the next night." He's so smart. He knows exactly how to prepare you.

Now with Bob, it's the exact opposite. He does all of his work in the rehearsal room. Once you're on stage in previews, he's supporting you with his mind, his thought, and his great love for Tennessee, but he's slowly checking out—bit by bit—on to the next project. His work is done in the rehearsal room.

Now Andrei Serban, with whom I worked a number of times at ART, never stops until the artistic director pays him to leave. Having grown up with that kind of direction, it's turned me a bit into a director junkie. I love to please my director, and sometimes it's a good thing and sometimes it's not. I miss that kind of absolute obsession that Andrei gives to a production. When he directed me in *Twelfth Night*, he had his own particular take on Viola, but he let me find it. I felt it was one of my most successful roles, in that I grew the most—not in the role so much, but I grew as an actress.

There's a particular rehearsal I remember vividly. It's the scene just prior to Viola's first meeting with Olivia, just before the "willow cabin" speech. He had me play it once like this little street tough, cock of the walk. I loved that; it was a lot of fun. Next time he said, "All right, now you must do it like Christ." That was not as much fun. In fact, when Maria says something unkind, I started to lash out at her, and he said, "What would Christ do? Turn the other cheek." And then he had me do it as a mixture of these things, and we sort of built this emotional tapestry. We put together this living, breathing person with all these conflicting emotions going on in her.

A very different experience was Paula Vogel's *The Baltimore Waltz*, which Anne Bogart directed at Circle Rep. I didn't have a bit of faith in it. I just didn't know what the hell it was. I had worked with Anne up at ART on a show that some people remember as successful and others remember as a disaster. I wasn't sure which way Anne was going to go with this, and I'd never worked at Circle Rep before. So it was a whole new kettle of fish. And I felt lost. Thank God for Joe Mantello, who was in it with me, and Richard Thompson. I remember saying to Joe at the end of the first week, "How do you think I can get fired from this production in the most graceful way?" Joe told me that he remembered from the workshop that the play had this peculiar heartbeat, and that if we just supported it and stayed out of its way, it would take over the evening. And he was right; it did. And Anne did give it this spectacular, simple structure in which to work.

Joe was remarkable. He played thirteen roles in the course of ninety minutes. He underplayed each one of them so brilliantly. It was hard to keep from cracking on stage. He would come on stage in the Dutch boy outfit with that blonde wig and his dark Italian skin, and I would just die. It's one of those shows that we all remember as a golden one. It was a delightful surprise, too, because people responded so well to it.

A Diverse Fifteen Years: Shakespeare, Sheridan, Chekhov, O'Neill

In 1980, I played Rosalind in *As You Like It* and Helena in *A Midsummer Night's Dream*. That was ART's first season, and I was twenty-three years old. Though André Belgrader cast me, I had no business playing Rosalind. I didn't know what I was saying half the time. But the older kids who had graduated from Yale would bring out their Onions' *Shakespeare Glossary* and help me with the text. It was a thrilling experience. In *Midsummer*, I had a cello playing under a speech of mine—that was a first. If I were to play Helena now, I'm sure I would approach it differently, but I don't know how because I really don't remember what I did. I was such a baby.

A few years later I did Lady Teazle in *The School for Scandal*. There was a difference in my approach to Lady Teazle because of the director. We had Jonathan Miller, and he's a big flirt. So in rehearsals I was made to feel like I was the cutest little coquette in town. That's the big difference. Suddenly I felt like a Lady Teazle because he had such charm. He's a genius. He brought this incredible knowledge with him. By the time we began the work, we knew the diseases these people were dying of, exactly how foul they smelled, exactly how long they'd live, exactly what the racial situation was in England as far as Jews were concerned. Jonathan needs no picture books. He can paint it all quite beautifully by himself. The background was a rich tapestry in which we created these people.

That same season I played Irina in *The Three Sisters*. That was a great production—truly beautiful. It was incredibly simple and pared down, and at the same time remarkably theatrical. Andrei took us to see Russian films so we would start to understand, or try to understand, the wonderfully manic-depressive personalities of these Russians we were playing. They really can be sobbing despondently one minute and then laughing hysterically the next. He wanted us to understand that those emotional shifts really can happen on a dime.

It was my first experience with Chekhov, and Andrei would read us Chekhov's letters. The handful of us in the company who were too young and inexperienced to truly appreciate Chekhov fell madly in love with him through his own voice. It was a breathtaking first experience with Chekhov, and Andrei was in a particularly mature place in his work—he had already had a great success with *The Cherry Orchard* at Lincoln Center. He said, "I know I'm a brilliant showman and I can make pretty pictures and dazzle people, and I don't want to do that this time. I want to present the text and let that be the focal point." And I think he pulled it off. Of course, it was tremendously theatrical. That is one of my all time favorite experiences. It was the watershed experience for me for a long time.

Playing Josie Hogan in *A Moon for the Misbegotten* was another remarkable experience, one I'll always cherish. Working on it had a profound influence on my life. It made me address my own drinking. I had many O'Neill late nights with the three men in the company—it was just me and the boys. The level of the drinking rose. And it was a few months after that that I stopped drinking completely. Jason Robards and I both learned a great lesson from O'Neill. You know, when they originally asked me to play Josie, I turned it down because of Colleen.

My love for Colleen Dewhurst is very well known. I talk about her almost every time I get a chance to speak. I saw her as Josie at Lake Forest in Chicago, pre-New York, in 1973. It was such a strong image that I couldn't see playing it myself. But I realized that *Moon* is not a play that's going to be made into a movie, and I thought, how else are young people going to see it unless contemporary actors pick up the gauntlet? So I did it.

I'm glad I did because Colleen's spirit was with me. Each night when I would look up at the moon in that beautiful, long transition from night until dawn, her face would be the moon. And on the nights when the catharsis had happened for me, she'd be smiling that amazing smile; and on the nights it hadn't, she'd be looking at me with a wonderful wink and a smirk that seemed to say, "It's okay, kid, try again tomorrow night. The gods forgive you."

BROADWAY

The Night of the Iguana by Tennessee Williams, directed by Robert Falls; *The Heiress*, directed by Gerald Gutierrez (Tony, Drama Desk, Drama League, and Outer Critics Circle Awards for Best Actress); *Angels in America*; *Our Country's Good*, directed by Mark Lamos (Tony nomination, Best Actress); *Macbeth, Stepping Out.*

OFF-BROADWAY

Goodnight Desdemona, Good Morning Juliet; *The Baltimore Waltz*, directed by Anne Bogart (Obie Award); *And Baby Makes Seven, Big Time, Light Shining in Buckinghamshire, I Am a Camera, The Philanthropist, The Importance of Being Earnest.*

<u>REGIONAL</u>
Pride's Crossing (The Old Globe Theatre)*; The Heiress* (Mark Taper Forum); *The Seagull, The Night of the Iguana* (Jefferson Award, Best Actress); *The Good Person of Szechwan* (Jefferson Award, Best Actress); *A Moon for the Misbegotten, Tartuffe, Cloud Nine, Cheapside, Cherry Orchard, He & She.* Founding Member, American Repertory Theatre, Harvard: *King Lear, Twelfth Night, Major Barbara, Caucasian Chalk Circle, The Serpent Woman, Life Is a Dream, The School for Scandal, The Three Sisters, As You Like It, Baby with the Bathwater, A Midsummer Night's Dream, Journey of the Fifth Horse.*

<u>FILM</u>
The Housesitter, The Big Town, Light of Day.

<u>TELEVISION</u>
Tribeca; Spenser: For Hire; Alex: The Life of a Child; Sganarelle.

"You have to be willing to be unloved, disliked, even hated as Patrice, because the impact of the final scene and the idea of forgiveness will be greater."

with Richard Clarke in *A Fair Country*

Photo by Ken Howard

Judith Ivey
How Believable Can You Be?

"Judith Ivey is one of the two most remarkable actresses I've worked with," said Mike Nichols, who directed her Tony Award–winning performance in David Rabe's *Hurlyburly*. (The other one? Meryl Streep.) "I would compare her," he continued in this March 1986 *Vanity Fair* interview, "to a female Al Pacino or Dustin Hoffman."

Like Pacino and Hoffman, Judith Ivey has shown great variety in her choice of roles. On stage, television, and films, she's been a hooker; a middle-class mother; an English upper-class matron; a middle-class Jewish sister from Brooklyn; a crusading district attorney; a Parisian street-waif who sings; a former Las Vegas card dealer; a Senator's obsessed wife who undergoes a public breakdown; a trailer-park party girl; a rich Long Island housewife cheating on her husband with, among others, Cupcake, the local policeman; and a lower-class Rhode Island wife who seeks sanctuary with her sister because she's just shot her husband to death. These roles, representative of the gallery of women Judith Ivey has brought to rich, subtle life, are a great source of our understanding of all women.

Her best roles, as she freely admits in her interview, have been on stage. In the last fifteen years or so, she's created some of the most complex, humorous, and emotionally shattering women in New York theatre. It would be impossible to forget—even if one wanted to—her endearing performance as the troubled East End chippie,

Josie, in Nell Dunn's *Steaming* (her first Tony Award); or her painfully funny performance as the cocaine-snorting stripper, Bonnie, in *Hurlyburly*; or Bea Small, a woman terrified because she's at the mercy of her husband for money at a time when almost everything in our country told us that women were second-class, in George Furth's *Precious Sons*; or Kathleen, a woman from a blue-collar background in Gloucester, Massachusetts, who must come to terms with her own human inadequacies in the home of her former high school teacher, in Israel Horowitz' *Park Your Car in Harvard Yard*.

Along with this great variety is Judith Ivey's total commitment to a role, a phenomenon I have seen close up, day-by-day, in rehearsals for one of her finest performances—Patrice Burgess, the angry, haunted heroine of Jon Robin Baitz's *A Fair Country*—the role she was playing at the time of our interview.

From the moment Judy first attacks the role, she begins developing an inner life that is intensely rich and complex. When she eventually walks on stage before an audience, accompanying her is a sharp-edged element of danger. It could be emotional danger, physical, spiritual, or all three. Whatever it is, it arises from an actress who is not afraid to take a risk. An example: Early in the rehearsal process for *A Fair Country*, Judy said to Dan Sullivan, the director, that she was unsure how far to go in her emotional breakdown at the end of Act I. She kept wrestling with the scene, pushing forward, pulling back, edging this way, that way. A few days before we moved into the theatre for technical rehearsals, during a particularly slow-going afternoon, Judy threw caution to the wind. In a confrontation with her oldest son Ali (played by Dan Futterman), she grabbed a rehearsal chair and flung it across the room. It was a terrifying moment. Later, in notes, she said to Dan: "As an actress, I don't know how much I can tear up." "As a rule," Dan said, with mock seriousness, "Tear up as much as you can before the stage manager comes over and says, 'Okay, Ivey, enough!' " No physical outburst of that kind happened again. But it was symbolic of the emotional explosion that finally did happen (which is discussed in her interview) and that galvanized everyone who saw it.

Finding out I wanted to act was a slow process. I was a successful art student from an early age—painting and drawing. I was taking college life-drawing classes when I was thirteen, while my mother finished her master's degree. Everyone expected me to do that. When I was seventeen, we moved. Though it was a small town and didn't afford many opportunities, there was the school play. I played Miss Preen in *The Man Who Came to Dinner*, and, you know, I was funny. I made the audience laugh. The bug certainly bit me that first time.

I was not going to college to major in theatre. In fact, a college professor who judged me in high school speech contests called my father who was president of a community college I was going to attend. She said, "Your daughter is very talented, and going to that school would be a waste for her." My father listened. I got a scholarship to a state university. I wanted to do a double major but the art school was so snooty they wouldn't allow it. So I ended up, in a strange way by default, majoring in theatre.

"Acting Is a Public Service"

When I finished I was too scared of New York, so I went to Chicago, not necessarily thinking that I would make acting a career. Somewhere in the second year of actually making money at it, I realized it was going to be a career. But the greatest affirmation was the curtain rising on my first Broadway show. It was such a dramatic moment. It's magical.

I think of acting as a public service—truly. It's therapeutic. I believe it's a necessity in life—not like food, shelter, or medicine. But after the basics are met, it's the next need. I see it as a privilege in the way that a doctor has the privilege of healing. That, of course, informs my choice of roles. Sometimes I feel, "I've got to do this," because the play says something that's important to me. I hate to use the word *message* because there are comedies that I've *had* to do—not to say that comedies don't have messages, but there the message is incidental to entertainment. So, there has to be something worthwhile, and I have to know I can contribute to the whole of the play. Though I don't think of *Steaming* as a play with a message, there was a morality to it. It had this integrity: You saw women naked, and it wasn't salacious, opportunistic, or gratuitous. That, in and of itself, was a statement I wanted to participate in. *Steaming* showed women the way they are, in all their beauty, without trying to capitalize on it, or exploit it.

I wanted to do *A Fair Country*, because the play is profound in what it says about the family and love relationships. It's profound in what it says about the world. I love how the microcosm of the Burgess family is a way to parallel if not be a metaphor for the greater family, which is people. Each character represents some aspect of the family of people and our behavior and how it impacts. I was taught to approach literature that way. I think of my professor and mentor every single performance, because he would have loved that aspect of this play. I feel it's a privilege to be part of literature that shows the world this way.

The message I got from the play that moved me immeasurably is the concept of *forgiveness*. One of the aspects of my training is that it's the *story* that's important, and another is that in telling the story, you can be unliked as a character. I knew that one way to approach Patrice is to play her as a total victim. And I think that's wrong. You have to be willing to be unloved, disliked, even hated as Patrice, because the impact of the final scene and the idea of forgiveness will be far greater. That someone can recognize, change, and find a way to say, "It was my mistake"—that's profound to me. It's part of the reason the world is so screwed up now—we are all so full of fear and pride and all these emotions that keep us from saying, "I made a mistake. I apologize." Just think of all the problems that would be solved if people could really regret.

Patrice Burgess is a lot like Bea Small, the character I played in George Furth's *Precious Sons*. What Robbie and George both captured was this profound dilemma for women: devoting their lives to caregiving, and then when caregiving is no longer necessary, who are they? If it is not part of your personality, necessarily, to be a caregiver—and I don't think it's genetic or gender-driven at all—therefore, what happens to those women when there's no need anymore? Bea Small in *Precious Sons* didn't really want a career. But she was so much at the mercy of the money her husband made that she was a walking, breathing package of fear: "What if it went away? What would I do?" Patrice is a perfect example of a woman who could have gone out and done something other than be a wife and mother, and yet she chose to do what she did. There was no gun to her head. And I think it was a detriment to the family. She was damaged and therefore her children suffered.

Second Lady, a one-woman show I did in the early '80s at the Production Company, is, once again, a woman taking second place, being in the backseat, totally controlled by the future of the man in her life. Her own personal outcome is based on that situation. This play had the added condition of the Senator who was running for President being such a driven man, wanting his success so badly that he put his wife out there with no awareness of the emotional state she was in—which is why she managed to fall apart in front of the group of women she was addressing.

I am fascinated by that—having been a young girl growing up in the '60s and '70s and having my consciousness blatantly raised. I look at my mother—she had a career, she taught school for as long as I can remember. She was not a woman who stayed home. And yet I saw repression in her. You know, I agree with what Terry Kinney said in your book: Actors have statements, and their work and choice of roles reflect that.

Pre-rehearsal: "I Use My Own Life"

Patrice Burgess was so personal to me that I found throughout the day, before we got into rehearsals, I would think, "Oh, this is like Patrice." Or, "Oh, that's a Patrice moment," or "What did I just do?" I began watching myself unlike I'd ever watched myself before, and a lot of it was the interaction with my children. If I were particularly irritated—which I certainly think is one of Patrice's difficulties—I would register it. How did I just do it? Why did I do it? What was the truth behind the irritation? More and more I use my own life as I think about a character, though I didn't used to. I think I used to step outside myself. I played many more characters that were not me. I'm not sure why it changed, but I think that I'm more fascinated now with "How believable can you be?" "How real can you be?" Can I make you actually believe that I *am* Patrice? I want to be so believable that people sitting in the audience will have a hard time wanting to be with me. I would say that I've changed as a person. I didn't like myself much, so I loved stepping out of myself and taking on a personality that wasn't mine. I might use pieces of myself, but I was much more comfortable playing someone I didn't really relate to. I liked observing them and playing them, but I didn't want to *be* them. Now, I am much more interested in what I can use of myself that will make you believe this character, and, therefore, believe the story.

I don't do a whole lot of research. If there's something in the play that I think knowing more about would add to my performance, I'll research. When I did *Hurlyburly*, because I was playing Bonnie who stripped with balloons, I watched women strip. I wanted to see the atmosphere that Bonnie would probably have been in. I don't think I would have gotten it otherwise. It wasn't something I could have imagined and been accurate about. When I did *Park Your Car in Harvard Yard*, I went to Gloucester, Massachusetts, and hung out and listened and got a feel of the place, just the "small townness." And that helped because Israel Horowitz uses real places and real people when he writes. I had exact houses, an exact high school, and stores in my imagination. Whether it added to my performance, I don't know, but it made it more interesting for me. I had a visual history in my brain.

When I was playing the lawyer in the film about Betty Broderick, I watched the real courtroom tape because I was playing a real-life person. It seemed good to study her. The things I picked up from her that I used helped me most in the quieter scenes, but for the dramatic courtroom scenes I had to alter her behavior because she was slow and methodical in the courtroom. It was undramatic and would probably have been boring.

The Rehearsal Process: Finding the Emotional Journey

When we start working on specific scenes in the rehearsal process, I tend to sit and say my lines out loud and imagine what the other person is saying. That's my homework. I go through the lines and twist them around and around. All of a sudden I'll hear something different. Ultimately, I like doing that in performance. It sets the pattern that it's never going to be quite the same. It's always going to vary.

I'm fascinated by the words playwrights pick, so sometimes in rehearsal I'll go through a scene once and accent odd words in a sentence. When we do the scene again, I'll emphasize other words. I'm trying to find out: *Why* did he pick this word? The one that I've been working on in performance most recently—I still haven't made it right—is in the first scene when she says to Gil right after she's arrived at the dig site:

It's actually really me.

Why did he write it this way? Right now it helps me to say,

It's actually [pause] really me.

I need that pause. Maybe she's going to say something and she stops herself? The pause makes it come out awkwardly. And that sets up the awkwardness in the scene. That makes sense to me. Sometimes, just for sheer variety and spontaneity, it's fun to pick a word and bump it and see where it takes you.

Ultimately, playing around with the words helps me find the emotional journey of the character. If I hit on a word and it triggers something and takes me to the next thing, I'll keep it that way because it's a good emotional trigger. If it takes me into an odd place, then I might not do it again.

To me there is music in everything. In comedy there's always music, so if you want a laugh there's an exact way that you can say something. The line at the top of Act II to Van Eden:

I looked down once and there was an entire interview with Madame Chiang Kai Shek on my frock.

If you break up that line, they won't laugh. So I'll play around until I find what rhythm makes them laugh. Remember last week. I started losing that laugh on—

I mean, if I had to listen to Philip Glass all day, I'd want to give blowjobs in the bike room, too.

I finally realized that I was giving too much emphasis to "Philip Glass." They started laughing on "Philip Glass" and didn't hear "blowjobs in the bike room." I realized I'm already telling them it's funny by giving everything the same emphasis. When I went back to *not* hitting "Philip Glass," there was the laugh. The music fascinates me.

The Director: A Real Collaboration

That phrase I used a moment ago—*emotional journey*—is something I look for. In the rehearsal process, working with Dan on this play, I pieced it together more than I have in past productions because of the nature of his direction. Because we're on the same wavelength, he would say, "Play it this way," and I'd do it. Then I'd feel what it did to me emotionally, and I'd know where the rest of the scene was going. It was almost like a piece of the puzzle being dropped in, and you say, "Oh, I get it." Things just kind of fell into place.

I adored working with Dan, though I didn't "get it" at first. I realized that he's here to tell the story, and that's why I'm here. Once I got my ego out of the way—because he is kind of thin on compliments—and recognized that he was using what I brought into the room, looking at the play, and asking, "Why are we writing it this way, Robbie?", it was fine. It is a real collaboration with Dan. It's so rare that people truly collaborate in this business that when it happens, you treasure it. Now, I don't necessarily agree that not giving a compliment every other day or so is a good idea. But I accept it in him because the reward is there. And it's a confidence in and understanding of the story you are here to tell. So that you enjoy being out there.

He leaves the door open in many places so that it never gets boring. He's not a director who sits on you and tells you to raise a finger at this point. And there are those directors. Some are equally as successful as Dan Sullivan. But I wouldn't want to work with them because that's denying me what I bring to the part. He respects you, and that respect is so important in going out there night after night and doing a good job.

Dan Sullivan and Mike Nichols, who directed *Hurlyburly*, are similar in that they both are there to tell the story. Mike would stop in rehearsal and say, "All right. What's the event here? What's going on now?" He'd let you babble, and then he'd summarize in one sentence, and you'd go, "Yeah, that's what I mean. Yeah."

They both have the unique talent of making it a collaboration, yet having their own personal vision, which is what I admire most in directors. I don't understand directors whose view is: "There's only one way to do it, and it's mine." Dan and Mike also have that unique ability to say, "I don't know," and not be intimidated by that fact. That's so wonderful.

Norman René, who directed *Precious Sons*, was much more instinctive, I think, than either Dan or Mike, and he relied heavily on what came at him. He was a man of few words, which made him somewhat like Dan. He was a question-asker. He rarely told you how to do something. He's probably the gentlest director I've ever worked with. He loved actors and he loved behavior, and he was very good at getting you where the behavior comes to life. I think of him as a therapist—he would literally inundate you with questions and let you find the answers. Therefore, the actors find the play. He was also very respectful of playwrights—to the degree that he would try and make it work rather than cut or rewrite it. Dan is different—very questioning of the playwright. "It's not working, Robbie. What do you mean by this?"

One thing I don't like is the director who makes the choice for me and dictates that that's the only choice. He/she might let me find the moment, but then he'll say, "That's it. That's what I want." In a way, he's a person who stymies creativity. Sometimes the director will sit on us, not allowing for any exploration. For instance, in the worst situation I remember, in the first three or four days of rehearsal, the director said, "That's the way I want it. Leave it that way." "We've still got three weeks," I thought. "Can we just play now? It's going to be so dead by the time we get to performance." But there was no playing around. To me there are a hundred possible choices for any given moment. How can we be sure so early? How can we make that decision now? In television, you have to be that way—make early, quick decisions. You have to work so fast that you don't have the opportunity to explore. So that's a good quality for a director to have in television.

"Everything Is Manifested by Our Behavior"

As I'm studying a role in rehearsal, the intentions of the character start, usually, as an unconscious thing. If I feel I'm not getting it, I'll get conscious about it. I use it like a hammer; it's a tool that I use if it's not instinctively happening. I rely on other actors a lot. And if it's not happening because they don't seem to know either, then I'll go back and say to myself, "Okay, let's play 'I hate your guts,' or, 'I love your nose,' and see what that produces."

The first scene in South Africa was the hardest one for me in *A Fair Country* because of the nature of the play itself: You do the end of the play first. So to fly back in time and decide who she was ten years ago is hard. To be honest, I'm not sure we've necessarily solved the whole problem. I don't know fully what I'm doing. Also I don't think I've been as daring as I would like to be. I've said playfully to various friends that I should come out and go for the jokes, and let *that* be the way Patrice is dealing with the problem. Play it like you're Bette Midler.

I've been described as a "physical" actress, and to an extent it's true. There's a physicality about this performance, and in that scene particularly. There's a gesture you pointed out to me last week: Just after Gil has left to get the drinks, I grab the fabric of my dress on my left thigh and crumple it. I gave that to myself as an exercise in the first couple of previews because of my confusion about the scene. I thought, "What if she is perfectly relaxed except for that gesture? What if she's acting like everything's all right and, literally, all the energy goes into crumpling the dress?" It was so useful that it's remained in the show.

I once had—oh, let's call it—an encounter with an actress with whom I was having a hard time working. I went to her dressing room and said I thought she didn't like me and I couldn't figure out what I had done to provoke this. And could we please talk about it because it was interfering with the work. Now, if you had only *heard* her reaction, you would have thought that she was the nicest person alive. She corrected me and said everything was fine. She didn't know what was going on to make me feel this way. She loved what I did as an actress. While she said all that in a very friendly, loving voice, she was frantically rubbing body lotion all over herself—it was so clear she was trying to rub the problem away. And I sat there and thought, "This isn't as bad as I thought—it's worse. It's insane." Her behavior fascinated me because, of course, there was a problem. Things like that always fascinate me—when we're saying one thing and giving ourselves away with behavior.

I just love how people deal with each other. Everything is manifested by our behavior. How is fatigue manifested? How is nervousness? How is dishonesty? It's why the words fascinate me. Which words would give away? Which words would conceal? If I really want to hide something from you, what am I going to do to keep it from you? Am I going to change the subject? Am I going to tell you, "No, it's none of your business."? Would I tell you in a nice way? Would I bark at you? So I watch people to see *how* their behavior shows what's going on inside. I was watching a girl read a sign on the subway today. She was just wide-eyed looking at it. It was like, "I can't believe what I'm reading." What does the face tell you?

Sometimes in the past, when I was working on a character, I would find a physicality first and work from that. For instance, Josie in *Steaming* was very clearly someone who loved her body. I honestly couldn't say that's how I felt about myself. I thought, How am I going to get over this? I decided to wear high heels all the time because it pitches your body in a certain way. I found that as I threw myself forward, threw my breasts out, stood on those pedestals, and looked at the sky, then she came to life. My tendency is to do the opposite—slouch—so I had to work against my own behavior constantly. Finally, it got where I could stand no other way. She just became a life force.

I did a television movie called *On Promised Land* when I was pregnant with my second child, Tom. Therefore, they made the character pregnant. The film took place in the early '60s. I remembered how women of my mother's generation always had a purse—it used to make me laugh—and I decided I wanted a purse for this character. Those women had a particular posture because they carried a handbag. Their arms, literally, were slightly raised up because they had a handbag on their laps. So, in preparation, I carried a handbag everywhere—on my way to the set, when I ate my lunch, when I left the set. To keep it up you have to carry it all the time. The handbag made that woman more pinched to me, and that's how she was as a person.

Actors in the Rehearsal Room

In rehearsal, I'm looking at the way other actors interpret their character and how that impacts me. I imagine what another actor is going to do. Then I'm intrigued with what their take is on their part of the story, and how it's going to affect what I'm doing. Occasionally in rehearsals I've been hindered by the way an actor worked. The one that comes to mind was where an actor had made a decision about his character that was completely derailing my character—not Judy's choices, but the choices of the character as written. It was virtually impossible to do the character's choices. I just stopped and said, "I'm finding it difficult to play what I understand, at this point in time, is the motivation behind my character because of what's coming at me. I don't know what to do with it. If there's a way, will you please show me? I'm at a loss." So it provoked conversation. Sometimes it provokes unhappiness. But for me, it's choosing what way you want to be unhappy.

"The Lack of Costume Was Far More Informative"

I'm very affected by the clothes I wear. I did a television movie recently, and my concept of the character was very different from the concept the producer had. He proceeded to go to the costume designer and completely change it. Since it was television and done very quickly, there was no time for a discussion. I would show up ready to do a scene, and here would be a completely different outfit than the one I had tried on. It was a 180-degree turn. I finally just had to show up and do it and try not to worry about it.

The wonderful thing about working on a character like Patrice with Jane Greenwood as the costume designer is that she listens greatly. I mean, I think she already has an idea of what she wants. When you work with someone like Jane, you just trust her. You don't have to worry about it. These costumes for Patrice work better than I thought they would when I first tried them on. There were some that weren't my first choice, and I remember thinking, why did I allow this to be a consideration. The caftan in the breakfast scene is a costume that now helps me in the scene because I *don't* like it. It irritates me, so I get more irritated as Patrice. It's filmy in a way that hints at the delicacy of Patrice's psyche.

I've sometimes had costumes that were like magic when I put them on. Almost all the costumes in a movie I did called *Hello Again* completely informed that character for me. Zelda just came to life when I put those clothes on. Also, there was an outfit I wore as Ruth in *Blithe Spirit* that made me feel like the belle of the ball. It was a day dress, but it moved in such a way that when I put it on, the style of the play itself came to life for me.

It's going to sound terrible, but the lack of costume in *Steaming* was far more informative to me than the costume—even though I loved my costumes. I remember the day in rehearsal I could no longer do the scene and wear clothes. By the way, there was no pressure to take your clothes off. I was the first one to do it. Now, you understand, once I was completely naked I went up higher than a kite. I said (with a cockney accent), "I can't think of a frigging word to say at this moment." That broke the ice and we were all free to do what we were going to do. It was so freeing when those clothes came off because that's what that East End steambath was about for my character. So being in your body was the most important thing.

Dialects: The Sound Informs the Character

I'll tell a story on myself. Someone early on in my career told me that I would never have much of a career because I had a terrible Midwestern accent, and that I certainly would never get hired to do any contemporary British plays. Maybe I should thank that person—maybe it motivated me. I was never quite sure if they were right or wrong, but it certainly drove me to make sure that I had as little specific accent as possible. Through doing that work I learned a lot about dialects.

Now, *Steaming*, once again, was one that I had never done—that East End, cockney sound. To get that just right lent itself to understanding Josie. It took you to a place that was much more specific than words on a page. And it's all part of the fascination with words and behavior, and that leads you to a specific geography.

In *Dolores*, a fascinating little movie about two sisters, I had to learn the working-class, Providence, Irish-Catholic sound. I had to, literally, go through that script word by word. It's such a hard accent. I wasn't entirely pleased with the results: the Providence sound is New York and Boston combined, which makes it difficult because none of the rules of each place really applies. They get twisted around. So even if you know certain rules about New Yorkese or Bostonese, you can't trust them.

Working on that accent, though, helped me with the character in *Dolores*, who is fascinating and wonderful to play—she's got all the emotions. The accent added to her class, where she fit in society. It added to the pitch of the character, her humor. Once I knew how to pronounce certain words, I could say to myself, "This is where she's throwing it away. This is where she's high," etc. You can just hear the music between the two sisters from that family and that place in society. The sound informs the character a lot.

A Mystical Experience

When I play a role, particularly in a long run, it does tend to seep into my life. For instance, when I did *Steaming*, I rarely wore clothes at home. It was very odd, and I was consumed with my body and what I looked like, as the character is. When I did *Hurlyburly*, I partied all the time. It was just part and parcel of playing Bonnie. It was a way of life that became my way of life. When I did *Precious Sons*, I was more fearful of everything around me. More than I normally would be.

Playing Patrice has been an education. I'm constantly looking at my own mothering, and what I'm doing and not doing. I worry about my children far more. I think that if I've learned anything from this play, it's the true meaning of forgiveness and the true meaning of humility. And I've learned it, in some ways, the hard way. I'm very proud of my work in this play, and I'm sometimes not very humble about it.

Acting, when it's full and true, is a mystical experience. Working on the breakfast scene at the end of Act I of *A Fair Country*, where Patrice has a breakdown, was very hard. I knew I had to go to an incredibly deep and, ultimately, mysterious place every night in order to do that scene. I knew it was a place that wasn't going to feel good, and I was afraid of it. Robbie does give you those great words that help a lot, but still you have to find it in yourself. I remember pushing myself through the scene and driving myself to see how far I could go. One day in rehearsal it triggered. It was so intense that my breasts tingled. (I shared

"I knew I had to go to an incredibly deep and, ultimately, mysterious place every night to do that scene. It was scary to take it physically to that place, but I knew it was right. I saw it had to be out that far, and now in performance it's knowing how far." Photo by Ken Howard.

Judith Ivey with Laurence Luckinbill in A Fair Country.

this with the other actors, and it became our joke. They asked me, "Did your tits tingle tonight?") It was scary to take it physically to that place, but I knew that it was right. I saw it had to be *out* that far, and now in performance it's knowing how far. I scared myself one night. I was afraid I was going to physically collapse, and that I wouldn't finish the play that evening.

I was talking last week with John Cullum and Keith David, and John remembered that Olivier once said that you must save a little part of you. You don't give them all, you give ninety percent. It struck a chord in me. This week I said to myself, "Let's see how far I can go and still keep that mysterious ten percent so the audience will wonder, What does she do when she goes into the house? What does Gil do when he follows her? Does he grab all the pills and the bottles? Let them imagine the next scene.

At the end of the show each night, I feel exhausted but fulfilled. I unfortunately have a keen ear. I hear everything from the audience. To me that's the other part of the process. This is a difficult play for people. They sometimes react to it in a way that does not allow them to embrace it. Sometimes at the end of the show I've been mad and unfulfilled because I gave it the full measure, and it didn't come back to me. I've learned that this is a role that, because of what happens to her, no one can ever give you back as much as you give. Discovering that was helpful.

Film and Television

Whatever I say about film, I have to preface it with this: I don't think I've ever been given a role in film that equals the complexity and depth of the roles I've had a chance to do on stage. You know, I've been incredibly lucky. The playwrights that I've worked with—George Furth, David Rabe, Robbie Baitz, Israel Horowitz, Alan Ayckbourn, Neil Simon, Lanford Wilson—have created beautiful pieces of literature that are immortal. And that's so meaningful to me—far more important than being a movie star. Working with great writers was always one of my goals.

In my estimation, the chief difference between acting on stage and acting for the camera is realizing where the eye is, and giving a performance for where that eye is—which I think I've only recently started to succeed in doing. That's the only difference to me. I think acting for the camera requires all the same skills.

Shooting out of sequence can be problematic. You might discover something after the fact, and because you've already shot the scene that succeeds or precedes it, you think, "Oh, I could have done this or that." It doesn't usually bother me because I've done my homework. I've mapped it all out. I've even come to the conclusion that the homework is not really necessary all the time because even though I've created the arc of the character, the way it's edited together is often not remotely what I worked out. In film, the arc of your character is someone else's decision. You can put it in there and hope they see it and use it.

There's really no difference, though, between the way I approach a character in theatre and a character in a film or on television. It's all about truth and believability. I really liked the character I played in the sitcom *Buddies*, the hard-drinking, former card dealer from Vegas, because there was a challenge in it, and there were many directions in which she might grow. In all the other series I've played the central character. The format of a weekly TV series is that the central character is the audience. You meet everyone through her eyes. In essence, you react to them the way she reacts to them. Therefore, they tend to make the central character more lifeless. More *beige*, I always say. It's not very interesting to act, particularly week after week after week.

The most important thing about a half-hour sitcom is the working environment. And the working environment on *Buddies* was terrific. Every once in a while I'd come up with a funny line and it would be put in. You felt it was important that you were there. I can't say that about every sitcom I've done.

"I Want to Be Entertained, Enlightened, and Educated"

I always look for the comedy in a role because I think it's more true to life. When I go to the theatre, I want to laugh, I want to cry, and I want to think. I've always said: "I want to be entertained, enlightened, and educated," and one of the easiest ways to entertain people is to make them laugh. And humor can certainly make a person more likable and more accessible. If I can laugh with you or at you, then it softens the edges. It opens a door. I think laughter is so human. No other animal laughs, and so I think it's unique to our condition, to our dilemma. And it's therapeutic.

I was in Chicago making a good living as an actress. I came here with a group of other Chicago actors to audition for soap operas. While I was here, I saw *The Royal Family* on Broadway with Rosemary Harris and Ellis Rabb. I laughed myself silly. I beat my legs with my hands to the point where my thighs stung. And at the end of the play, I was sobbing. I have tried to steal that bit of Rosemary Harris—where she collapsed on the floor—several times, and I've yet to do it. After all the laughter, there was the stillness of that last moment. Incredible. She is one of my idols because she changed my theatrical life. She gave me the inspiration: "I want to do that. That's what I've got to do." It was the experience of live theatre, and it can't be reproduced anywhere else. I never forgot that whole afternoon, and it's twenty-one years ago. And it's certainly one of the reasons I came to New York and why I'm here now.

BROADWAY

Park Your Car in Harvard Yard (Tony nomination, Best Actress); *Blithe Spirit*, *Precious Sons* by George Furth, directed by Norman René (Drama Desk nomination, Best Actress); *Hurlyburly* by David Rabe, directed by Mike Nichols (Tony and Drama Desk Awards, Best Featured Actress); *Steaming* (Tony and Drama Desk Awards, Best Featured Actress); *Piaf, Bedroom Farce.*

OFF-BROADWAY

A Fair Country by Jon Robin Baitz, directed by Daniel Sullivan (Outer Critics Circle nomination, Best Actress); *Moonshot and Cosmos* by Lanford Wilson (Obie Award), *Pastorale, Second Lady, Dusa, Fish, Stas and Vi, Design for Living.*

FILM

There Goes the Neighborhood, Love Hurts, Miles from Home, In Country, Everybody Wins, Sister Sister, Hello Again, Brighton Beach Memoirs, Compromising Positions, The Woman in Red, The Lonely Guy, Harry and Son, Dolores.

TELEVISION

Series: *Buddies, Down Home, Designing Women, The Five Mrs. Buchanans, The Critic.* Films: *The Shady Hill Kidnapping; We Are the Children; The Long, Hot Summer; Decoration Day; A Woman Scorned: The Betty Broderick Story; On Promised Land.*

Will they kiss? "Even though Anna was feeling a similar thing to the King, my defense mechanism started to go up. Now that doesn't happen so clearly. The moment has changed since the opening. It's become more sexual. But there can't be a kiss because it goes to another place."

with Lou Diamond Phillips
in *The King and I*

Photo by Joan Marcus

Donna Murphy
The Serious Songstress

Culminating in her glorious performance as Anna in the 1996 revival of Rodgers and Hammerstein's *The King and I* (for which she won her second Tony Award as Best Musical Actress), Donna Murphy has shown a wonderful and quite rare diversity as a performer in musical theatre. A few instances that bring back very fond memories:

—Seeing her for the first time on a New York stage in a short-lived off-Broadway musical called *Birds of Paradise*, in which she played a plain tomboy stagehand so convincingly that one had no idea how stunning she really is.

—The sheer pleasure she radiated playing Edwin (and Alice Nutting) when she took over the title role in the Broadway musical *The Mystery of Edwin Drood*.

—In 1991, being astounded by her booming be-bop voice when she blew the roof off the theatre as Rose of Rangoon, the comically tortured amnesiac ("Danger is my middle name. Now if I could only remember my outside names") in *The Song of Singapore*.

—Her unusually haunting performance of Vera in Rodgers and Hart's *Pal Joey* at the Huntingdon Stage in Boston. In a largely reworked version of the 1941 musical, she sang the sultry "Bewitched," to her naked sleeping lover, Joey, while she was lying in bed in a filmy nightgown smoking a cigarette. As she finished the song, singing, "I'll sing to him, each spring to him,/ And long for the day when I'll cling to him, /Bewitched, bothered, and bewildered am I," Joey awakens and they resume their lovemaking.

—Her galvanizing presence as The Whore in the opening and closing sequences of Michael John LaChiusa's musical take on *La Ronde*, called *Hello Again*, in which her performance made me rethink how much I'd taken for granted about "the world's oldest profession."

—And no one could forget her astonishing Fosca in Stephen Sondheim's *Passion*, which made everyone who saw it—even those who didn't like the musical itself—wonder at the subtlety, depth, and grace of a performance that was almost unbearably moving.

All of this diversity comes from the fact that Donna is, in the words of writer/composer Mary Rodgers, "the best actress in musical theatre today."

While she can do miraculous things with the words and notes of any song—listen to the recent recording of *The King and I*, and you'll hear a subtle terror in her voice as she sings "Whistle a Happy Tune" to her son Louis—a very important fact about Donna Murphy is this: She could never utter another musical note and still have a rich career, because she is a fine dramatic actress. Anyone who saw her frighteningly hilarious performance as Dorothy Trowbridge in James Lapine's *Twelve Dreams* at Lincoln Center a couple of seasons back will know what this means. Donna made very bold choices about this eccentric, wealthy, somewhat laughable woman (assisted, as she describes in the interview, by the costume designer, Martin Pakledinaz), but the inner life she created made those choices work. There was not a moment when you didn't believe she was a living, breathing human being you might meet tomorrow at a cocktail party. In fact, with all its eccentricity the performance was so subtle, it didn't look like acting at all. And isn't that the way it should always be?

A Single-minded Purpose

I think I knew I wanted to be an actress when I was a little girl. My mother tells me I asked her for singing lessons when I was barely four. I remember making up stories and enlisting whatever kids in the neighborhood were available to act in them. Then when I was in kindergarten I was Goldilocks without a wig—believe it or not!—in "Goldilocks and the Three Bears." A desire to act seemed to be present early on. This was always what I was going to do. In sixth grade, I had a remarkable drama teacher, Judy Kahan Beck. She was unusual for junior high school—very alive, creative, unrestrained in her imagination and in her approach to things. She put together a show called *Full-fledged Spirit*—poetry, literature, and music from many sources. It was about recognizing your potential as a human being and what you have to offer the world. It was so exciting to be collaborating on something.

As a child, I think acting was an outlet for my imagination. I have a memory from the end of "Goldilocks and the Three Bears." We were dancing to rock and roll—it was a contemporary Goldilocks; the curtain came down, and I was stuck in front of it. I remember feeling both humiliated and excited. Everyone was laughing and clapping. I'm sure that that moment, and that feeling, in some way continue to motivate me. There was a sense of focus, or purpose, that I had from a young age. It was almost too simple for me. In fact, later, at a time when I was questioning whether I wanted to actually continue to act, it made for a huge difficulty because I had always had such a single-minded purpose in my life.

It was a period when I was questioning acting as a career on a number of different levels. I didn't know if physically or spiritually I'd be able to continue doing what I was doing. So my body forced me to reconsider. I took close to a year off. In the long run, it was a blessed time for me. I came back with, let's say, a renewed sense of purpose and a shift in perspective. It may have been there before, but I had lost sight of it.

Choosing a Role: The Material, the Character, and the Story

I think my reasons for wanting to play a certain role have been different at different times in my life. The decision to do Mrs. Anna, for instance, was complicated for me. When I was approached about her, I was still doing *Passion*. This was the first time in my career that anybody had talked to me about doing something a year from now or two years from now. That's a luxury but it was something I wasn't comfortable with. My first thought was, "Why do we want to do another *King and I*?" It didn't seem it had been that long since the last major revival with Yul Brynner. The Dodgers (who produced it) said, "Here's the libretto," and they gave me the original recording with Gertie and Yul Brynner. I had, in the interim, listened to the recording with Julie Andrews and Ben Kingsley and been blown away by it. I went home, after a lovely meeting with the Dodgers, and it was on the list of possibilities, but not foremost. If I was going to do a musical, I was generally interested in doing something new.

Well, I read the libretto and was astonished by it. I was moved and surprised at how it read like a play—how complex a character Anna is and he is, of course. What an opportunity for two interesting characters to be alive on stage together. "I have to seriously consider this," I thought. As an actress who sings, I know that roles like this are rare. So I had several meetings with the director Chris Renshaw, who was very bright and open-minded about who Anna could be. He had had very specific experiences as a British person in the East, and they seemed to be informing his take on the play. That interested me.

Another complicating factor: I didn't initially see myself as Anna. I didn't have a picture of me inside of it—not to say that I always do with a character. But it's certainly easier with a new piece. You don't have some preconceived idea of what it should be. So, I would say that I wanted to play Anna because of the material and the character—and that there was such a strong story to tell.

Deciding to do the role of The Whore in *Hello Again* was different. I got a call from Ira Weitzman, who was then the musical development director at Lincoln Center. He said, "Donna, it's Ira. We're doing a week-long reading of a new piece based on *La Ronde*. Graciela Daniele is directing, and the guy who wrote it, Michael John LaChiusa, is really talented. You'd be great in this character of The Whore. You'd be in the first scene and the last, and part of the Ensemble." Well, it was too good not to do. So I kind of fell into The Whore. Then when I heard the actual material—the way Michael John jumped around in time, using archetype, the way he played with gender even, and the score—I fell in love with it. So exciting.

This was one of the first musical pieces I'd worked on in the period when I had decided to come back to work. I remember coming home from rehearsal during the workshop and saying to my husband, "If I could exist in a rep situation like this, with a company of people who create this way, with the kind of desires they have in terms of work, creativity, and just plain fun, I could be happy the rest of my life."

The character of The Whore was fascinating. She was a metaphor for so many things. The writing itself was very strong, but because I understood certain things at that point in my life, I knew I could imbue her with an emotional life that would make those metaphors palpable. You know, you can talk about this stuff up the wazoo, but if you don't get it, feel it, and convey that feeling to an audience, it doesn't matter. Anyway, she was a giver, without expectation, which people don't understand, and they judge it. To get to play a woman like that was a gift, especially at that time. So in this instance, I did it for the character, the composer, and the chance to work with Graciela.

With the role of Fosca in *Passion*, there was never a moment's hesitation once I knew it was an opportunity to work with Steve and James, whom I'd admired fervently for years, and a chance to create this daring, unusual character. When I first heard about the project, I was doing the workshop of *Hello Again*. At the time I was going up for a lot of whores in films—three films actually. Because I was The Whore in *Hello Again*, when my agent said to me about *Passion*, "It's a Sondheim-Lapine project," I said, "Is she a whore?" And he said, "No, she's a nineteenth-century, consumptive neurotic." And I said, "Oooh, even better." They gave me a few scenes and the only existing piece of music for her. I'm frustrated with situations where I can't see a full script, even for an audition. It's hard for me to do the work, without a full script—no matter how small the role. But when I saw that piece of music and the lyric, Fosca came to me. It's what I call her first aria—"I Read"—her meeting with the captain. And it was all in that piece of music. There's so much information in those lyrics, and it's so evocative. There was this little section in my insides that started to feel like her.

It was both an emotional and intellectual response. I felt like I got her, and I got her here [pointing to her head] and I got her here [pointing to her heart]. And I liked her. Her struggle moved me. I'm still surprised when people tell me they didn't like her. I never understood it, and that doesn't come from that ego feeling, "How could someone not like a character that *I* created?" I don't mean that. What she's dealing with is so large you have to admire it. The lyrics move me even now:

> I do not read to think.
> I do not read to learn.
> I do not read to search for truth . . .
> I read to dream.
>
> I read to live
> In other people's lives . . .

It's about finding the whole truth, and about going beyond the confines of your own life. The information about Fosca that's in the song is tremendous.

Stimulating the Imagination: Researching Mrs. Anna

I sang from the time I was a little girl. I saw acting and singing as separate but equal. I never thought I would do just one of them, and I never thought I would only do them together. In fact, when I was in high school, I did all the musicals and all the plays. I also did competitive speaking, which most people think of as debate and oratory, but when I did it, it was primarily dramatic interpretation. We'd each do a ten-minute cutting of a play and play all the characters. I learned a lot about acting during my high school years, in terms of recognizing theme, structure, and delineation of character. I was the queen of accents—a very bad Meryl Streep. It was a great experience. The actress part of me was not a sideline to the singing. I'm trained as an actress. My training as a singer came very late—in the last four years actually.

I always start my research with the script itself. Even when it's a musical, there's still a script. I then read two of Anna Leonowens' memoirs and also the novel that Margaret Landon wrote about her, *Anna and the King of Siam*. This was all before I decided to do the piece. I also did a lot of reading about Thailand. It was part of my decision-making process.

Later, I read things that were written about Anna Leonowens and a book that was written about her son because there was a lot about her in it. The research was fascinating and confusing, because there were people who challenged her telling of those stories and questioned her version of not only her time there but of who she actually was. All of this research was useful in the long run, but at a certain point I found myself confused about Anna. It would be one thing to have all of this information on a project that was being written while you were rehearsing it. You'd have a dialogue with the writers and the director, and you might inform some of the choices. Now *The King and I* is an existing work that has been interpreted a number of times. I didn't want to do it just for the sake of doing it.

A turning point for me was talking with the director, Chris Renshaw. He kept saying, "I'm not afraid of what's dark in her, and I know you love exploring the darkness in characters." He described the time he'd spent in the East and talked about his experience on the dock of Thailand, coming into Bangkok the way Anna does. He explained it was filthy, disgusting, and the smells were revolting. There were animals and snakes literally crawling at your feet. He said that Anna's singing "Whistle a Happy Tune" must have been her way of overcoming this situation and rising above it. That put a new perspective on that scene for me.

Research stimulates the imagination, but it doesn't tell you what to do.

Fosca: Understanding the Physical Situation

I read the novel on which *Passion* is based. I started to watch the film and had to stop because it was so different from what I'd started to see in my mind's eye (later I did see the film). Because Fosca was such an avid reader, I read literature from that time. I wanted to know what she might have read. Some were novels that were referred to in the script.

That was very important to me, because Fosca read the novels that Georgio gave her. They were incredibly romantic novels, and I mean very romantic, very sexual, though not pornographic. If a man gave me one of those books and said, "Read it," and I was open to any kind of suggestion—and God knows Fosca was hungry for it—why wouldn't she ask, "Who is this man who reads this kind of literature, responds to it, and wants to share it with me?"

An important aspect of my research for Fosca was understanding her very particular physical difficulties. Her physical situation was such a large part of who she was. I never felt that her physical symptoms were not real. She was not just an hysteric. I knew enough, even from my own experience, that, yes, something can be motivated by stress or trauma, but still when you have the symptoms, there's a real physical thing that happens as a result. There was no judgment on my part there. I had to find her physical life so I talked to neurologists about different kinds of seizures, and I read a lot of Freud and Breuer, particularly about women. The range of symptoms from illness was huge.

Pre-rehearsal Work

The kind of homework I do, before and once I'm in rehearsal, depends on the particular requirements of a role. Once I made the decision to do it, the research for *The King and I* included dialect work because I think it's important to get a head start. It's very necessary to get that music in your ear. I worked with Deborah Hecht, who's a phenomenal dialect coach. I wanted to start with her as soon as possible. Because I'd been working vocally on it already, I wanted the sound to become second nature to me. I'd been working on the songs with something of a British accent. But I felt I didn't know how this woman talked. When I started to work with Deborah and the accent changed a bit—Anna had spent time in Wales—it changed some of my vocal work because I realized some of the vowels were different than I'd thought, and I had some new choices.

You know, the music for *The King and I* was strangely difficult for me. I started singing the songs before I knew for sure I was going to do it. I began working with my voice teacher because the score sits in a very in-between place for my voice. It's the most traditional musical theatre I've ever done. So I felt trapped a bit in terms of freedom of sound. It was tricky for me. As we worked, I thought, "I don't think I'm going to sing this music in a special way." I've never thought I had a great voice. It's interesting and an emotionally communicating voice. I have a large range, so I'm able to do a lot of different things.

It's very important to me that the songs be completely integrated within the scenes. It makes me crazy when I hear a song that doesn't come out of a scene. I'm fortunate because in this show, the writing, for the most part, is really there for the songs to come out of the scenes. As the performer, you have to justify this question: "Why wouldn't I just say this? Why sing it?" You have to find the reason why speaking is not enough. We have to assume the emotion is so large that you can't just speak. You either have to go more inside—and music can make it more private—or you have to go outside. The song is always a monologue that's underscored. One of the fundamental teachings of my voice teacher, Joan Lader, is that you speak when you sing. Sometimes when I think that I've made a great sound, she'll say, "You're not speaking." And she's not coming from an acting place, she's talking about a physiological use of the voice. Anyway, I want going from speaking to singing to seem perfectly natural.

The Rehearsal Process

In rehearsal, in preparation for working on the scene, say, where Mrs. Anna asks the king about the house he's promised her, first, I read the scene many times. I would make whatever choices I could make at that point about the circumstances leading up to the scene: knowing that she'd arrived in Siam, how long she had been there, where she'd been living, what her day-to-day existence had been like, what was mounting up in her leading to the moment when she enters the room to confront the king. (In this version, she breaks into the room. I loved that idea.) I'd have thought about what she expects to see in the room versus what she encounters when she gets there. Beyond that, I might make some notes about intentions. I don't usually plot the intentions, moment by moment. But every once in a while where I have to go in for something fast, like a film, I might. But even there I usually rely on my first instinctive response to it.

What I like is this: At home, I've made decisions about what precedes the scene, who the person is going into it, what she wants. Then in the actual rehearsal I just play the other side of the net. Sometimes, for whatever reasons, what's on the other side doesn't motivate you, so you have to work a little differently. I've studied in two different situations—both descendants of Stanislavsky but in approach completely different. It's two different sets of tools. I prefer to be text- and imagination-oriented, and just be very clear about what the person wants and needs. Occasionally, though, I do use private memories and substitutions of things.

The rehearsal process with Lou Diamond Phillips was very good. Our first meeting was sitting around a table reading the Moses scene. I felt that the most important thing was that the king be a complicated man, and I wanted to feel sure that whoever played it would be someone who's really there on the other side of the net every night. I want the security of knowing that if I start playing something with a little different rhythm to it, he's going to be there responding to it, not just hitting his marks. In that first reading, I knew the potential for that was there. I was affected by Lou, not just as Donna, but as Anna might be. We tried everything with each other. It was sexual, it was intimidating. He was like a child I wanted to slap or cuddle. There were so many things going on in him that I felt he'd be a real partner.

Lou is very different from me in the way he works. By his own admission, he's more comfortable with someone making a suggestion and he'll try to find a way to do it that way. I tend to question more, and if something is not comfortable the second or third time, I'll say so. He was very patient with the way I work. He once said, "I'm lucky to be working with someone like you, because otherwise some things might not get asked." He was, and continues to be, very generous.

That new moment in the show, the "possible kiss" during the "Shall We Dance" number, has been talked about a lot. It's not in the text. We worked on it very carefully. What's written is a reprise of the polka. Chris had this idea that the dance kind of slows down on itself, and they become more and more wrapped up in each other. It's the kind of thing that's great if it just happens, but it never really happened. So we tried slowing down with the music going faster, and it felt somewhat manufactured. The choreographer told us that there are various ways of holding your partner in doing a polka. He demonstrated a way that the king might hold her. So we tried it once with Lou coming over to me and putting both his hands around my waist, and what we do now is really an improvisation of that. We all agreed that they shouldn't kiss. But the whole moment has changed since the opening. My response used to be a "don't touch me" with my hand coming up, or a gesture of "I don't think you want to do that." Even though I was feeling a similar thing to him, my defense mechanism started to go up. Now that doesn't happen so clearly. It's become more sexual. But there can't be a kiss because it goes to another place.

In discovering who Anna is, I felt it was important to decide what her relation with Tom, her husband, had been. Chris and I talked about the fact that Anna had really thought that the love part of her life, the sexual part, was over. That door had closed. Later, I decided that her reverie about Tom in "Hello, Young Lovers" is true, that her love for him had been true. It was different from what she feels about the king. But I felt very strongly that she shouldn't be a woman who had never been sexually pleased. That would make the moment with the king the wrong kind of moment.

Importance of Making Choices

My experience with *The King and I* is a good illustration of choices and how you can reevaluate and change them. I don't like making early decisions about what kind of person she's going to be, although occasionally I'll have a sense of rhythm for a person, or a sound, or a walk. I'll be reading the script and a picture will fly into my head. Someone may wear a hat that will trigger something in my imagination. It's all about triggering a whole picture. Little details accumulate. By the end of our rehearsal period, I had made some basic choices about Anna. But during tech week in the theatre, I realized that I was on the wrong track. I wasn't dismissing the work I'd done, but it wasn't working for me. I'm not the kind of actress who can just bury it. I have to replace it with something. I had to say to myself, "This is not right." You always continue to try to delineate what the person needs, what the person wants, what the circumstances are. But I was questioning the choices I'd made about who she was. I was at a point where I was so panicked I actually thought of dropping out.

So for the first time in my life I brought in a coach. I was so jammed that I didn't know how to shake it up by myself to come to a clear picture. John DeLuca was a friend and a director, and I'd known him a long time. Originally, I called and said I was having trouble. We talked for a while and it was so stimulating that I asked him to come to rehearsal. He would watch rehearsal, then on breaks in my dressing room we started a dialogue. I can give you many choices for any one moment, and sometimes I need to try them all. So in that room with that one person, I would try this choice, I'd try that one. I gave him maybe ten different Mrs. Annas. He knew what my concerns were, and he was able to keep the big picture in mind. I wasn't so desperate that I'd take anything. He threw some things at me and I'd say, "You're wrong." Sometimes I'd be right that he was wrong, and sometimes I'd be wrong. We had debates and arguments. We knew each other so well that we didn't have to worry about hurting each other's feelings. I knew that you could tell the story of this woman in many different ways, but I felt I had to serve *this* telling. If Oscar Hammerstein were there, it would have been easier, too, I think. But it was with John that I finally began putting the pieces together.

Maintaining a Performance

It's so important in a long run to be fresh and yet faithful to what you came to in rehearsals. I reread the scipt about once a month, and I review the situation of the play. I go back periodically to Anna Leonowens' memoirs. Occasionally, I have to have a conversation with myself reviewing what the character wants in a situation. Beyond that, it's really trying to stay as open as possible. Also, I try to be accepting of the kind of tidal quality that comes with being in a show for a long time—knowing that I'll have a "dry night" here and there. But I find when that happens, I'm often moved in another place, or provoked by something else in another moment that's completely new. I try not to spend time thinking of the moment that's passed and what was disappointing about it. If you do that, you miss whatever's coming at you.

Costumes: An Extension of Who You Are

Your costumes are what the person is inside of. They can dictate how you move, certainly when you're dealing with hoops and corsets as in *The King and I*. You need time with a costume to deal with how it changes you. You want it to become second nature as you deal with the trappings. That's just the structure aspect. Then if you're talking about the choices someone has made as to how they clothe themselves, they have to be in sync with the other choices you're making about who the person is.

I hadn't thought of this before, but deciding on what the character should wear is part of your technique. I remember Stella Adler saying, "Your talent is in your choices." I don't see how you could be responsive to every other detail and then feel, "Costumes are not part of my job." As I said, the clothes are just an extension of who you are. Of course, you must be respectful of the designer and what they have to bring, but you're the one who's going to become the character.

When I saw the photographs of the costumes from the production in Australia, I was pretty sure they weren't going to be right for me. The director assured me we were going to redesign. He and I had an initial conversation. The designer, Roger Kirk, came over and we spent several days talking about how Anna should look. My feeling was that there needed to be a progression: when she first appears, she's covered, armored almost, and then as the play goes on, more and more of her is exposed until after "Shall We Dance."

First, we decided that Mrs. Anna had been in mourning less than a year. We didn't want her in black but felt it should be dark. So Roger came up with this really deep midnight blue. Since she's traveling, all the accoutrements would make her very covered—all of this is how she's chosen to present and armor herself. The next dress, which in Australia was white, seemed too vulnerable to me. I wasn't sure what color it should be, but I felt she should still be armored. Originally, we talked about steel gray, but the dress in the next scene, the schoolroom, is black and white and reads kind of gray, so we came up with that sort of aqua, green-bluish dress. There's a steeliness to it. It's the same color as my eyes, which nobody would know except me. But that might be a reason Anna would have chosen it.

Fosca: Nobody Is Going to See Much

You could hardly ask for a more different look from Anna than the clothes for Fosca, designed by Jane Greenwood—a goddess. Her attention to detail is incredible. I felt about Fosca: Nobody is going to see much because she was ashamed of her body. She'd already been told it wasn't a pretty sight. That little bit I knew, and I also knew she was someone who would have to be in clothes that were comfortable. So I felt she shouldn't be corseted. I also felt I should appear as flat as possible. However, I knew I had to be able to sing and breathe properly, while holding tension in my body for her. So Jane, who is remarkably inventive, came up with what she called a "corselet," which was cotton and ribbed and compressed me a bit. She said, "Fosca may have no money, but she's still a lady who came from refinement and would have a sense of what's proper." For instance, Jane designed a little handbag that Fosca carried when she went to the garden. There were other little details. There's a bit of lace on one dress that Jane felt might have been something she had before she was sick, when there was still some money.

Then we decided that nothing of Fosca's should be pressed. She probably spent a lot of time in bed, and she might easily take a nap in what she was wearing. Jane is a wonderful technician with clothes. For instance, I looked a little too wide in one dress. So Jane did two things. She moved the shoulder seam over to make my shoulders look more narrow. She felt that the sleeve should be slightly shorter to expose the wrist bone and the hand.

Dorothy Trowbridge: The Clothes Defined Her

I wanted to play Dorothy Trowbridge in James Lapine's *Twelve Dreams* because I loved working with him on *Passion*, and the combination of James and Lincoln Center (the producers) was like coming home. I loved the character, but I was concerned about her being another neurotic woman who had a traumatic memory, even though the physical trappings couldn't be more different from Fosca. Dorothy is one of

"There was a kind of arrested development in her womanhood, and so whatever she wore would be accessorized within an inch of its life. There was no room for her true self to be revealed."
Photo by Joan Marcus.

Donna Murphy as Dorothy Trowbridge in
Twelve Dreams.

those people we'd meet and make a very quick judgment about. I thought, "Wouldn't it be interesting to play one of those women and reveal, literally, the little girl within her." I felt she could be funny, too.

Martin Pakledinaz is a great designer, and those clothes helped me understand who Dorothy was. First, we felt she's a person who keeps reinventing herself. Each of her scenes has such a different tone to it in terms of her personality. Marty had this idea that she might be fascinated by women movie idols. He said, "Wouldn't it be interesting if she had her clothes designed based on movies she had seen, but that there's a personality to each of the looks?" My feeling was that, because of what had happened to her, there was a kind of arrested development in her womanhood, and so whatever she wore would be accessorized within an inch of its life. There was no room for her true self to be revealed.

Dorothy smoked, and the smoking had to do with not showing herself. There's a haze of smoke around her all the time. I also felt she should have lots of props. I wanted her to always be busy, because if she sat still she'd have to think about herself, and that would be too much for her, actually not possible.

Approaching Character: Television and Film

I like to find as full a history for the character as possible in whatever medium I'm working. Of course, the history changes because there are things I discover in rehearsal, even sometimes in performance, that make me reassess what I thought before. It helps to have that history to operate from, and then you can shift things around if you have a flash of something you'd like to add.

Even in situations like television and film where you have to work fast, I like to give myself some kind of background, or world in which to exist. A good instance is *Murder One*. I read the pilot script, saw the shooting script, and there was very little information about this woman, Francesca Cross. She was the wife of the first prime suspect, played by Stanley Tucci. She had been away for the weekend at a spa. I remember the day we were shooting. "What does she know?" I asked. "We don't know," they said. "Could she have been involved?" "Possibly," they said. So what do you play? I had only one scene per episode so each show was like an acting class for me. I did decide that in every episode she would have some secret she was keeping, and it wasn't the same from week to week. *Murder One* was a great acting exercise for me in how to approach something quickly and with depth.

Someone Had to Be Benny, a film I did for HBO, was about a right-to-die issue. I played the mother of a very ill young man. I did my research, studied everything written about the case, watched a feature on the family that was on *20/20*. I kept watching the footage of the son. I'm not a mother, but I am a stepmother. Some of the emotion is primal in terms of the desire to protect your child, so primal that I was instinctive about a lot of it. The family was Cuban, but the director, Juan Jose Campanella, had decided not to deal with that. However, I did decide to give her a slight New York accent since they had spent so much time here, and it added to her specificity as a human being.

We shot it in two weeks, so I had to rely on my instincts for a lot of it, though I had worked it all out for myself chronologically. I had graphed things out on paper so that when we shot—and we shot out-of-sequence, of course—I could just let things fly. It was the first time on film I'd played somebody who was out there emotionally. Mostly I've played more contained women.

The Decision to Study Voice

I have always sung, and I've sung a lot. My first professional job in New York was one of the back-up singers in *They're Playing Our Song* in 1979. Many times I had almost started to study, even on occasion taken a lesson. Most people seemed to focus on what was wrong with what I was doing, and I was nervous about trying to study while I was working. "How do I go messing around with this and getting rid of old habits while I'm singing every night?" I thought. So I always said, "When I'm doing a play, I'll study voice." Well, most of the plays I did then were out of town so I couldn't study, or couldn't afford to, so I kept putting it off.

When I was doing *Song of Singapore*, I started to have vocal problems and a variety of health problems. The pattern with me was I would get tired or sick, try to push through the show anyway, my cords would swell up, etc. Several times the doctor I'd been seeing over the years said to me, "You should see this vocal therapist. She's a teacher as well, but she's very analytical about the physiological aspects of what you're doing." I was kind of brought to my knees on this one, so I went to Joan Lader as a patient. Initially, we had to work on just speaking. I still have to work on that because I had bad habits in speech, and they carried over into my singing. I have a lesson right after this.

I think another reason I was afraid of studying voice was that I was unsure of being technical about something that I had always been instinctive about. I didn't want to approach songs from a place of sound, even though I was certainly aware of sound. I tended to think of sound in terms of evoking feeling, suppporting some idea of character, not about the most beautiful or the most well-supported sound, or the most blow-them-away sound. A certain part of me is regretful that I didn't have the technique earlier on, but then I think that I wouldn't have other things that I have now.

BROADWAY

The King and I, directed by Christopher Renshaw (Tony Award, Best Actress in a Musical; Drama Desk and Outer Critics Circle nominations); *Passion* by Stephen Sondheim, directed by James Lapine (Tony Award and Drama Desk Award, Best Actress in a Musical); *The Mystery of Edwin Drood*, *The Human Comedy*, *They're Playing Our Song*.

OFF-BROADWAY

Hello Again (Drama Desk nomination, Best Featured Actress in a Musical); *Twelves Dreams* by James Lapine (Drama Desk nomination, Best Featured Actress in a Play), costumes designed by Martin Pakledinaz; *Hey Love: The Songs of Mary Rodgers*; *Song of Singapore* (Drama Desk and Outer Critics Circle nominations, Best Actress in a Musical); *Privates on Parade, Showing Off, Birds of Paradise, A . . . My Name is Alice, Little Shop of Horrors*.

REGIONAL

Miss Julie, *Pal Joey*, directed by David Warren, book by Richard Greenberg; *Dangerous Music*, *Are We There Yet?*, *Oliver!*, *You Never Know*, *Ataria*, among many others.

FILM

Jade

TELEVISION

Series: *Murder One*, *Law & Order*, *A Table at Ciro's*. Daytime: *Another World*, *Loving*, and *All My Children*. Films: *Someone Had to Be Benny*, *Passion*.

"The strong emotional connection I made with Alma, and Williams, was frightening so I was resistant at first to play her. . . . But, I've never had writing that allowed more of the mystery parts of myself to emerge. Williams' writing has tapped into parts of me that I didn't even know about before."

with Harry Hamlin in *Summer and Smoke*

Mary McDonnell
That Mysterious Place I Go

I remember quite vividly—though it was eighteen years ago—the first time I saw Mary McDonnell on stage. It was in Sam Shepard's Pulitzer Prize–winning *Buried Child* at the Theatre de Lys (now the Lucille Lortel). She was playing Shelley, the giggly, hippie girlfriend of the youngest son. She was the only character on stage not part of that strange, hidden family of the American West, and she seemed to be walking, talking, watching, and listening at a different speed from everyone else. She was a human forty-five in a roomful of long-playing. The performance had such a distinct emotional rhythm that it seemed to emanate from her very soul.

The first time I observed Mary McDonnell in rehearsal was when she took over the role of Heidi Holland in Wendy Wasserstein's *The Heidi Chronicles*, a play I stage-managed first at Playwrights Horizons in 1988 and also when it moved to the Plymouth Theatre on Broadway. Mary was the final Heidi in the Broadway production, during the summer of 1990. After having been in rehearsal with three other Heidis—Joan Allen, Christine Lahti, and Brooke Adams—and three other full companies, I wasn't looking forward to this experience with only rapt pleasure.

What a happy surprise it was when I discovered new, important, and unquestionably relevant things about the play and about Heidi herself *because* of the way Mary looked at and interpreted the role.

On the first day of rehearsal, I saw that this is an actress who engages all of herself, all the time—mind, body, and spirit—as she works. She can focus on a scene with a concentration that leads her to find out—and us her audience to discover each time—what the character is doing in the scene at that particular moment, and what this tells us about the character throughout the play.

Mary McDonnell's presence on stage is mesmerizing. Even when she's doing nothing, we are in complete empathy with her. You can actually *see* her thinking and listening, and the way she listens helps you understand not only what her character thinks, but what the person she's listening to thinks. I remember the day in rehearsal when I realized—as they were working on the emotionally complicated wedding scene, Act I, Scene 5—that I understood Scoop Rosenbaum, her super-hip, upwardly mobile boyfriend, better because of the way Mary-as-Heidi listened and responded to him.

Mary goes after understanding what she calls the "overall journey of the character" with so much energy and precision that it leads, I believe, to the distinct emotional rhythm she finds for each character. It was there in Shelley. It was there in the emotionally uptight Leslie in Dennis McIntyre's *National Anthems*, in the ferocious Linda Rotunda in *Savage in Limbo*, and in the newly wisened Cheryl in Emily Mann's *Still Life*. I will never forget Mary's performance as Alexandra, the heroine of Darrah Cloud's stage version of Willa Cather's *O Pioneers*. She found a rhythm for this courageous frontier woman that was supported by a beautiful Swedish dialect. The way she said Alexandra's line, "I am so tired of having a body," was enormously touching because it revealed the woman's entire life.

This ability of Mary's was especially clear as she worked in rehearsal on Alma Winemiller in *Summer and Smoke*—the 1996 Roundabout revival of Williams' play, the first New York production of it since the 1952 off-Broadway one that launched the career of Geraldine Page. Because Mary discusses her rehearsal process for Alma so clearly and in so much detail in our interview, I will stay away from any specifics here. But the integrity with which she approaches the turbulent emotional life of Alma Winemiller is one of the chief reasons she is able to get to what she calls "that mysterious place I go."

"A Means of Understanding the World"

My freshman year in college I took an introduction to theatre course as an elective. I was a liberal arts major. It was during that class that I discovered theatre. What happened to me when I started to read plays was quite profound. I think it was the first time that my brain understood how to view the world. In other words, I started to think in a completely different way. My particular intelligence was stimulated through reading plays. I found that if I was reading dramatic literature in the form of a play, I began to understand character, situation, social situation, history, communication, philosophy—all the areas of life that one is supposed to be studying. A play was a means of my understanding the world. I started to comprehend and actively think about the world in a way that I never had before.

When I choose a role now, I think about what it says about the world—it's almost a prerequisite, though it's not usually conscious. Unless it says something about the world, or society, or the individual in society, or the politics of the time, or the gender politics of the time (a subject that's become very important to me), then I don't respond emotionally anymore. I just don't respond.

How I came to play Alma Winemiller is an interesting progression in self-knowledge. When Todd Haimes, artistic director of the Roundabout, called and offered it to me, I said I would read it. When I hung up, I thought, "I remember that play. I'll never do it, but I respect Todd so I'll read it." I had seen an ill-informed production of the play in college, and I may not have even read it. So my impression was not correct. When I read it, I was brought to my knees with humility, devastated by the truth in it. As I finished the play, in tears, in my bed, I said, "I can't play this. It's too sad." I called my agents to say "no," and they asked me to have lunch with David Warren, who was going to direct it. Because I'd been so moved by it, I said, "Okay, but I really don't know if I can do it. I don't need this pain." David and I talked for several hours. We had such similar impressions of the play. I realized that it was an opportunity that I was afraid to take, which is why I was saying no.

The strong emotional connection I made with Alma and Williams, with all of them really, was frightening, so I was resistant. When I spoke to David, I realized that he and I saw a lot of the humor in the play. We saw a lot of what makes the play about survival. I felt much better about the possibility of doing it. I don't think I could have done it with a director who had a less joyful approach to it.

Pre-rehearsal Work

Usually, I like to feel that I have the part I'm about to rehearse somewhat under control. But because I'd had such a strong emotional response to *Summer and Smoke*, I knew I had to leave it alone, and not try to figure out *why*. So I did something I don't normally do: started memorizing words. Alma is a mammoth role, she talks for days at a shot, never stops, and I knew we had a short rehearsal time. I had to do something to prepare, even though I didn't want to mess with my understanding of it. So I memorized her big speeches.

Usually, however, I do a lot of investigating and question-asking. I like to write questions on the blank page of my script, opposite the page with the text. I just write questions, but I don't necessarily try to answer them. I like to have my questions ordered. For instance, a character might say, "I didn't mean that." My question might be, "Is this literal or is this a layer?" I start questioning the layers of the character and the psychological makeup of a particular moment. This helps me understand whether I'm playing the truth at that moment or not.

I prefer my understanding of a role to be largely unconscious. When I first started out, I used to break it down very specifically, because I was so frightened. I was afraid not to have all these things answered. That's one way my technique has changed over the years. I try now to leave it as mysterious as possible.

It's very helpful to have a set of actions to rely on, because they launch you, and often launching is all you need. I discover most of my actions on my feet in rehearsal. Almost everything I can rely on as playable—which I have to have by the time I'm performing—I discover on my feet, and then I might jot it down. For instance, I might write, "I found out that I was doing this action or that action." I won't set out looking for it because to be playing an action from the beginning of the rehearsal process limits what you discover.

As the run of a play goes on, the actions don't seem to change so much. What seems to grow and change is the route to the fulfillment of the action. The way you get there seems to become more textured as time goes on. It's not as clearly cut a path as when we first begin. Sometimes in performances, something becomes clear and you feel you've been doing something wrong. In fact, I had one just the other night in *Summer and Smoke*. In the Fourth of July scene, one of my first lines to John Buchanan is: "You home for the summer?" Now, up until then, I knew that line in the context of my larger action—which was to converse, make contact, not be flustered, to keep talking so that one of those "enormous silences" won't slide in. At that performance, it occurred to me that she doesn't know how long he's home. "You home for the summer?" was actually a question. And it was so much fun to have it be that simple. It also makes the route clearer and gives it more texture.

Before rehearsals, I do background work. I like to understand a human being's time period—when they grew up—so I understand the social constraints that were on the person. I like to understand the kind of life they were living. I was impressed with the information David brought into rehearsals. It placed us in terms of the time period. Looking at that map, we saw where Glorious Hill might have been on the Delta. I've done a number of shows that took place at the turn of the century, so I've researched the period before. But the article in which women speak about what marriage was like—what they thought it would be and what it turned out to be—was really fascinating. It made for an understanding of the place of women then. Also, the other versions of the play we saw. Being able to look at things not included in the play, the outtakes so to speak, was useful too. It just gave us more layers.

Working on Dialect

When I have a specific accent, as I do with Alma, I work on that before rehearsals. Carla Meyer had helped me with the Louisiana accent for *Passion Fish*. I had three sessions with her before I came here. I knew we'd have Deborah Hecht during rehearsals but I was afraid I wouldn't have enough time in rehearsal to get as particular as I needed to get. So I decided to get going on it with Carla.

The work I do on an accent while I'm thinking about the character enables me to pretend that I'm not working consciously. When you're working on an accent, you can get all this information on a character and all this technical information about how to speak a line, but pretend that all you're doing is working on an accent. Technically, I worked on how to say a line, how to say a word, how to emphasize a phrase, and what word I was going to stress. That technical information goes into my brain and stimulates something in the creative-imaginative area, and things happen even while I'm sleeping.

The accent teaches you things about the character. For instance, at the third session I had with Carla I was going through some of the speeches, trying to understand the sound, and something clicked in: I heard Alma's tone of voice, I heard some of the vocal places I would go with her. It was as if Alma was coming in, and I started to understand her. This was the beginning of my understanding how big she was, the size of this woman. I mean by that, the size of her soul, her heart. I certainly undertsood the size of her journey before, but I didn't really understand the size of the gal I was playing until we started working on the accent. She has a huge effect on John Buchanan because she's a huge person. This doesn't mean she's not subtle or complex or in pain herself.

When I first read it, I realized the import of her actions. Here is a woman who, first of all, is a singer in a small town. She's highly verbal, has a great vocabulary, is flamboyant, eccentric. This is not a timid soul. If you sing in public, you can't be—you're passionate. She's having anxiety attacks because her doppelganger is so close to the surface. Alma takes unbelievably courageous actions for a woman living in 1916. First of all, she tells John the truth in the first scene. She says, "You hurt my feelings, you've succeeded in your purpose, let me go." She continues to tell the truth. She blasts through every rule—she calls him up, goes on a date with him, grabs his hand first. She does a lot of things that even today women don't have the courage to do. I thought, "How have we misread her and why?" You know what? Tennessee wrote this play a long time ago, and a lot has happened to women since then, and to men's awareness of women. He was way ahead of us with her, way ahead of us. He put her out there, far more than his other female characters. No other Williams heroine has courage like Alma's. Look at that beautiful speech of hers in Scene 6 when they're on their date at the casino. John asks her a question, and she says, "I'll answer that by asking you one. Have you ever seen, or looked at a picture of a Gothic cathedral?" Her imagination is amazing.

> How everything reaches up, how everything seems to be straining for something out of the reach of stone—or human—fingers? . . . The immense stained windows, the great arched doors that are five or six times the height of the tallest man. . . . To me—well, that is the secret, the principle back of existence—the everlasting struggle and aspiration for more than our human limits have placed in our reach. . . .

She lifts herself out of a situation she can't deal with by relating it to something large in the universe. She's so outspoken, and you know something? Audiences are really getting it. The way we're doing this play seems natural to me. Nothing has to be worked at. The proof in the pudding is I haven't had one night where it hasn't been there—and you know the level at which I'm playing this. If I were playing her as timid and repressed, I would be exhausted now. My state of mind would be, "Get me to a mental ward." She's so alive and vibrant.

You asked me last week where is that mysterious place I go to get Alma. I'm not sure I can describe it, and I'm almost afraid to investigate it until I'm done playing her. You know, I've never had writing that allowed more of the mystery parts of me to emerge. Williams' writing has tapped into parts of me that I didn't even know about before. I didn't know Williams was the right writer for me until I did this play. And I'm not sure all the roles are right for me.

Working on the Overall Journey

The kind of work I do at home the night before a rehearsal changes from role to role. If I'm playing a huge role, I don't do a lot of specific preparation the night before. That's because I'm working on the overall journey of the character and I want to be surprised by the discoveries I make. If I'm not in rehearsal eight hours a day with the whole thing, and I'm coming in to work on a specific scene, I'll sit with the scene the night before and read and reread it, mostly to let it work on me. I don't like to do a lot of work on it. That just traps me.

I try to let the play make me laugh, or cry, or let one of the other characters take my attention. I love to do that the night before—let another character absorb me. Then when I'm in rehearsal, I'm much more interested in them, which your character needs to be. Because of the nature of the role of Alma, I was completely obsessed with John Buchanan—who he is, what he wants, what his role in life is. Alma is a bit of a muse for him and she carries his well-being in her, on a soul level. I also got very taken with Nellie. And then, eventually, once I was courageous enough, I let in Alma's mother's pain. That took me a while.

When another character takes you, it's an interesting tradeoff. Eventually it pays off for you, but that day in rehearsal may be hard because you lose your own continuity. They're affecting you so much that your own action becomes less specific. To me, this is one of the more interesting aspects of the whole process.

If there is physical work to be done, I love doing it. For instance, working on *Passion Fish*, I spent a lot of time with physical therapists. I went to a center in Los Angeles, and they were really gracious to me. In the paraplegic wing of the hospital, they taught me how to work wheelchairs, how to do physical routines that May-Alice would go through. Sometimes, too, unconsciously I start to create situations in my life that are in the script, and I swim around in them a bit.

Now obviously for *Dances with Wolves*, where I learned to speak Lakota, I had to do many other things. We had three weeks of rehearsal in South Dakota. Every morning we went to horseback riding school early because it was too hot to do it later. We'd go out to the ranch and we'd ride bareback. That's when I got nicknamed Dust in Her Face. All the guys would take off, and I'd be back there going really slowly with my trainer—I wasn't crazy for riding bareback at first. Then we'd go to archery and gun school. We'd go back to the hotel, clean up, and then go to dialect class. We'd sit in a banquet room in the hotel, and we'd work with our Lakota coach on the language itself, talking to each other in the language, hearing each other, and understanding what's being said. Later in the afternoon we rehearsed. That was our day, for three weeks. Working on *Dances with Wolves* was extraordinary, a completely wild experience on every level.

But, you know, whatever I do as preparation depends on the project itself and what the requirements for the particular role are.

Working on a Difficult Scene

I love directors' brains and all their possible ideas. In rehearsal, David Warren would often say something about Alma that was so intelligent it would stimulate me. Even things the director says that I don't necessarily pick up on for the character are still stimulating. I love it when a director provides me almost a shadow, so I know that somebody is there with me. I'm like Peter Pan with the shadow sewn on. I'm not scared to go where I have to go—into these strange places and possibly fall into these holes and make mistakes—as long as the director is there with me. I don't like feeling alone.

Working on Alma, most of the places I fell into turned out to be kind of usable. When we worked on Scene 6, the casino scene, we had all sorts of discussions because it's such a gnarly scene—getting clear

"This dress is Alma's best shot and she takes it. She knows it's not quite right. It's the perfect dress because sometimes Alma feels beautiful in it, and sometimes she feels like a little girl. The dress actually helps me now."
Costume design
by Martin Pakledinaz.

Act I, Scene 6, "The Casino," Summer and Smoke.

about what Alma is after and what John is after. It was fascinating and a very difficult exploration. It takes a lot of stamina for the two actors to learn how to fulfill their own individual objectives *and* to be affected by the other whose objective is wildly different. Where I get into trouble as an actress is if my controlling brain gets too much information, I immediately make adjustments. It's a weakness of mine. Some actors can sit around and discuss the scene ad nauseum, get up to work, and have what they need. If I get too much information, my brain gets in a power struggle, I start making adjustments to win, and I lose the innocence. So, in this process, to protect myself from having too much information, I couldn't listen to some things that were discussed.

The hardest thing for me in rehearsing Alma was making sure that Mary didn't intervene to protect Alma from what Alma had to go through. It was quite a situation with Mary standing in a room with two men—David Warren and Harry Hamlin happened to be the ones—discussing this play about a woman. Quite often, the situation got Mary activated, and I'd have to leave the room because she'd want to start defending Alma. There was a lot of trepidation in that room; it was somewhat like being in a committed relationship where the two people involved are going into one of those all-night sessions that scare the living daylights out of you. But that's where we had to go. We made it through, and it paid off. It's very joyous because there's such trust between Harry and me on stage.

"Other Actors Are Like a Banquet"

I can't wait to see what other actors are going to do. I can't wait to be affected by them and to feel what they're going to make me feel. For instance, Adam LeFevre as Roger Doremus in *Summer and Smoke*. I didn't know how important the relation of Alma and Roger was until Adam informed me who Roger was in my life. Roger is not as easy for Alma to give up as one might assume. Early in Act II, in the scene where I learn that John's engaged to Rosa Gonzales, I sit down and say, "Why would he do such a thing?" Sometimes I look up, and Adam's looking at me with such compassion, it's almost unbearable. As we perform the play, I'm learning that because of what Adam as Roger brings to me, there's another whole layer of missed opportunities: soul mates who can't be together. Miss Alma has been so preoccupied with John Buchanan that she can't see the gift of Roger. For me, other actors are like a banquet.

"The Dress Actually Helps Me Now"

Every aspect of the production affects me deeply. But if I don't have on the right costume, I just can't do it. It's like having the symptoms of the flu—you know something's wrong but you don't know what it is. If you don't take care of it, though, it's going to get worse. When I don't have the right costume on, I feel a little sick.

That's partly what made for the change in the first costume for Alma. First, Marty Pakledinaz's costumes for Alma are brilliant. As with every show, though, the costumes had to evolve. He had given me this gorgeous white lace coat, which went over the dress. The idea was great—this formal uprightness for Miss Alma as she sang in public on the Fourth of July. But I felt so *strong* in that coat that I felt I could just walk all over John Buchanan. It didn't allow me to be as frightened as I knew I had to be, or as vulnerable. Now this was a problem because of what the coat did to *me*—on another actress it might have had a very different effect. It's so beautiful I've asked Marty to save it for another role.

The costume I wear to the casino is an interesting one to discuss because of what I learned about myself. I kept saying, "Marty, I know it's beautiful, I know it's right, but I just don't feel right in it." The cut was changed to make it more appropriate. Everyone thought it was perfect. Finally, I realized what it was: It was Mary getting in the way. There's something almost a little inappropriate—she doesn't have the right dress for this date. It was Mary saying, "I want the right dress." Once I realized it was Alma's insecurity, I was fine. This dress is Alma's best shot and she takes it. She knows it's not quite right. It's the perfect dress because sometimes Alma feels beautiful in it, and sometimes she feels like a little girl. The dress actually helps me now.

The hardest part of the play to do is the beginning of the Fourth of July scene. It's technically the hardest, verbally—to just talk and talk and talk. The emotional twists and turns in it are not as clear to me as some other parts of the play. Also, the audience is getting used to the play: trying to place this eccentric woman, the southern accents, a period that's not our own. They're also absorbing a lot, because a lot of information is coming their way. And Alma has certain behaviorisms and affectations that not only get displayed but are talked about, all at once.

A couple of times Harry and I have slowed down the beginning of the scene because the audience is not wholly with us. That's one of those consciously instinctive things that happens because we all have to get into the same room. I don't think live theatre really occurs until actors and audience are in the same room. For many reasons, some audiences have been there from the first moment and some have been reticent and have a "show-me" attitude. When you get a "show-me" audience, you instinctively take a little more time. When the audience is with us, you can just fly with it, because they're so ready to romp.

Alma's Eccentric Behavior

Alma's gestures and her behavior mostly just happened in the re-hearsal process. But Williams is very clear about this: There is eccentric behavior in Alma but she is not a foolish woman. So that was the acting dilemma. You don't want to back off and be timid about the gestures. (I'm not like that anyway—it's not fun.) On the other hand, she's got true dignity. So I read and reread his stage directions. Normally, I cross out all stage directions, but I really absorbed the ones about her behavior. Had I been playing Alma without knowing what he wrote about her flurried gestures and vocal mannerisms, I might not have come as fully into her physical life. I didn't plan a thing, though. It just started to occur.

I know there's been a lot of talk about the final moments of the play. Williams says something about Alma gesturing to the angel. He uses the words "valedictory salute." That made me laugh. "What the hell does that mean?" I thought. "This isn't a timid moment. It's not a moment of 'I'm off to kill myself and ruin my life.'" What I got from his description is a woman who's going to take on the angel as opposed to being haunted by her forever. So my response to the angel really came out of what he says. If you go back to the scene before and look at what Alma says, this is a woman opting for life, so she's saying to the angel, "I'm going to defy your restrictions." That's a strong gesture and a strong decision. I don't feel she's victimized by the angel. The final moment is about a woman finally deciding to risk living, as opposed to a woman standing at a window, in her corset, sadly fanning herself.

A few days ago, I was thinking of *The Heidi Chronicles*, and that there's a similarity between Heidi Holland and Alma Winemiller for the actress playing them. Like Alma, Heidi requires tremendous verbal energy, because she was a smart woman and loved words. When I was working on Heidi, I studied some of those words technically, particularly the art lectures at the beginning of each act. How many actresses get to say "Sofonisba Anguissola" on stage? Of the many characters I've played, Heidi and Alma are most alike. Heidi is kind of a reborn Alma. She's like an Alma for the 1980s. Both of them are very smart, way ahead of the time they live in. Therefore, they're not understood and have a sense of isolation because of that. They didn't fit in, you know, and they didn't fit in for a unique reason: They were more on the ball. Of course, there are large differences, too.

"The Warm-up Starts Her Moving in Me"

One of the most important things in maintaining a performance during a run is what you did in rehearsal. If your rehearsal process has allowed you the security of discovery, then your performance will stay fresh. If your rehearsal process has been controlling, repressive, and right-wrong, you'll have a hard time maintaining it. That's the first thing: to continue to allow discovery so that it will stay fresh. For me personally, I also take tons of vitamins, minerals, and herbs, and I have acupuncture.

Maintaining a performance like Alma Winemiller is like athletics to me. It's not unlike doing the fall football season. When it's over, you're going to fall apart, but while it's going on, you're going to maintain it with your trainer, masseuse, and whatever else it takes.

The warm-up on stage before the show is really the key for me in a play like *Summer and Smoke* because it unlocks her voice and her sound in me. I don't really talk like Alma. In everyday life, I use an eighth of my vocal range. Alma uses all of her voice. Vocally she goes everywhere. I have to unlock that before the show every night. Otherwise, I can't let her out. The warm-up starts her moving in me. It's really essential, more so than any other part I've played.

An Artistic Association: Working with Emily Mann

A lot of what I know as an actress I learned working with Emily Mann. An interesting thing about Emily is that when you talk about your character with her, you talk about it privately, on purpose, to protect that thing. It's different from the chemistry that David Warren encouraged in our rehearsals: that very open discussion. However, as David goes on in the process, he becomes more protective of space, and as Emily goes on, the discussion emerges more openly.

When I first started working with her, I felt a connection pretty quickly. Once I'd done *Still Life*, which she wrote and directed, I knew I wanted to work with her again. That one was rewarding for two reasons: First, it was a gift to have the opportunity to address Viet Nam on any level because of the tragedy it created in so many lives: what it was in the time of my college years and then its aftermath. This was somewhat like what I felt in my first theatre class—my way into the world—and in *Still Life*, there it was on every level. Also, to be able to play an Irish alcoholic—you know, I've known a few—was very important. To explore the humanity of that situation was such a gift to me. And finally—on a purely technical level—it was a wonderful opportunity to do a play that breaks the fourth wall. It was very exciting.

Emily has many strong qualities, but in my experience, her greatest is the ability to allow you to go anywhere. She may not think it's the right choice, but you won't know that for a while. She'll let you correct it on your own, if possible. She'll just absorb what you do. She provides an amazing container. The Jungians talk about the fact that as a parent you have to provide the container for your child to grown in. Emily is an incredibly maternal director and provides that container. In rehearsal, you're in her petri dish, and you can grow any way you want. She gently nudges you. If she wants you to change something, she'll say, "Uh, Mar, do you think that maybe . . . I don't know, but I was just thinking, maybe you could . . ." It used to make me laugh, because by the time I'd worked with her three or four times, we finally got to the point where she could simply say, "Mar . . .", and I'd know what she meant.

Because we did *Still Life* and *A Doll's House* each twice, I'd say those two opportunities were particularly fulfilling because we were able to go further and further, director and actress, together. We had the opportunity to work on them for the amount of time that one should.

Exploring a Character in Film

When I work on a character in film, I do approach it somewhat differently because it's film. I can't be as mysterious about it because I don't have the rehearsal process. I have to make more conscious choices. And you have to be ready to shoot because often you don't rehearse at all. So I have to make the choices more consciously, and do a lot more imagining, pretending, and acting out on my own before I get on my feet.

For instance, John Sayles, who directed both *Matewan* and *Passion Fish*, doesn't rehearse. He very deliberately works on a small budget and shoots quickly. But it's all right, for a couple of reasons. One, the writing is brilliant. *Passion Fish* is a great script about the relation of two women. To me, he's our greatest screenwriter, and he's a great director as well. The second reason: On both *Matewan* and *Passion Fish*, I received from John a handwritten letter—pages and pages—about the character. It's like a composition. You get who the person is in John's mind. Of course, you've already got a lot because of the scripts. But the background information—who they are, what their parents are like, their socioeconomic situation, how they grew up, situations that may have helped form this aspect or that aspect of them—is terrific. It's like being with the writer when he creates it. A lot of the stuff you spend weeks in rehearsal trying to make up your mind about, he just sends to you.

Most films are shot out-of-sequence, and I deal with that through a lot of writing. My script for a movie looks a lot different from my script for a play. I do a lot of connective-tissue writing, so that if I'm supposed to shoot the second-to-last scene on Tuesday morning and I shot the scene prior to that three weeks ago, I may have jotted down some things in my script that I learned. You almost have to graph it, so that when you go back and you're ready to shoot the scene that comes right after this, you look at what you wrote. It's the link for your imagination. I write in different colored pens. If there's an aspect of the character that I want to understand in the whole script, I might follow through on that aspect in red, another aspect in blue, another in green. That way, if you suddenly feel, "I don't remember the red throughline," you've got it there. You don't have to keep taking in the whole script to get yourself lined up.

Because you shoot out-of-sequence, acting in a movie is more scientific. You don't have the rehearsal time or the entire event each night to give you the throughline. You have to be more systematic in order to connect the elements of that life.

Another difference between acting on stage and in film: In theatre, by the time I get my costumes, I've already experienced the entire character from beginning to end. I've played it out, lived it. In a movie, I get my wardrobe well before I've opened my mouth, so oddly enough I work from externals. (I expect we're all forced into it by the nature of the thing.) Externals come first. I have to think through an emotional throughline, make choices by myself. Then I get my clothes, and I incorporate that into my picture as I'm working on it. I even write my costumes in the script so it all becomes integrated before we shoot.

"Little by Little It Gets Discovered"

Sam Shepard's *Buried Child*, which I did in 1979, was the beginning of my working the way I work now. Robert Woodruff's ideas as a director were liberating to me. Instinctively, I knew as an actress that it has to happen in that room, at that moment. I rebelled, again instinctively, against bringing in certain kinds of thinking, preparation, and substitution. Robert Woodruff used to say, "Find it now, find it now, find it now." We'd start off rehearsal with the entire cast tossing a basketball around, surprising each other with fast and slow, up and down. That created the moment, and it was the beginning of my being liberated to work with unconscious freedom. So it's not that my way of working has changed: It's just deepened and gotten more confidence. For me, a role gets created by what's happening that day. Little by little it gets discovered, and then every night the audience creates a little more freedom. I got a career out of *Buried Child*, and it's because it was the first time I was led to work truly from myself. I was lucky—it was a great play that won the Pulitzer Prize. For me, that experience was like I'd finally stepped into my own world.

BROADWAY

Summer and Smoke by Tennessee Williams, directed by David Warren, costumes designed by Martin Pakledinaz; *The Heidi Chronicles* by Wendy Wasserstein; *Execution of Justice*, written and directed by Emily Mann; *After the Season*.

OFF-BROADWAY

Three Ways Home, Savage in Limbo, All Night Long, A Weekend Near Madison, Buried Child by Sam Shepard, directed by Robert Woodruff; *Still Life*, written and directed by Emily Mann; *Letters Home, Black Angel, Death of a Miner, Twelfth Night*.

REGIONAL

O Pioneers, National Anthems, A Doll's House directed by Emily Mann; *The Three Sisters, Stitchers and Starlight Talkers, Death of a Miner, Red River*.

FILM

Independence Day, Mariette in Ecstasy, Passion Fish, written and directed by John Sayles *(*Academy Award nomination, Best Actress*);* *Sneakers, Grand Canyon, Dances with Wolves* (Academy Award nomination, Best Supporting Actress); *Tiger Warsaw, Matewan, Garbo Talks*.

TELEVISION

Series: *High Society, E.R., As the World Turns*. Films: Arthur Miller's *The American Clock*; Willa Cather's *O Pioneers* by Darrah Cloud; *Hawk, Courage, Money on the Side, The Morrow Castle, Shakespeare and Love*.

"The way I approached Rose was different from the way I'd approached any other character. I started with the realization— 'The feeling I have for Jimmy is the way Rose feels about Troy'—and I created her by reacting to him."

Photo by Ron Scherl

with James Earl Jones in *Fences*

Mary Alice
Always Have a Secret

Sometime in the fall of 1980, a good friend of mine called and said he wanted to give me what he described as a "very special theatre experience." A few nights later, heeding his explicit directions, we met at 7:45 outside Theatre Four on West 55th Street, then the home of the much respected Negro Ensemble Company, a number of whose productions I'd seen before. That night I experienced for the first time the artistry of Mary Alice.

Her performance as Rachel Tate in the original production of Charles Fuller's ferocious and sad comment on urban life, *Zooman and the Sign*, so touched me that I have never missed the opportunity again to see her on stage in New York or its environs. The specific moment that grabbed me and the entire audience and left us limp with spent emotion—you could actually feel us in Ms. Alice's emotional sway—was when she took clawing vengeance on the man who'd slain her twelve-year-old daughter and then, without any obvious transition, transformed her hatred into pity. It was so powerful that it was almost unbearable. In everything I've seen her do in the sixteen years since then, Mary Alice has never failed to please, surprise, and sometimes amaze me. No matter how small or large the role, when she walks on stage, a potent force is with us.

Every once in a while, I will remember—each time with renewed emotional impact—the moment in August Wilson's *Fences* when

Mary Alice as Rose Maxson, holding the illegitimate baby daughter of her husband Troy (James Earl Jones) and another woman, looks him straight in the eye and says with utter simplicity: "As of right now, this child's got a mother, but you a womanless man." The night I saw it, the line was greeted with a cheer (as I heard it often was), because Rose stood at that moment for all women who have been oppressed by thoughtless, selfish men everywhere. That moment would be a fine one for any actress, but in Mary Alice's extraordinary hands, it was sensational. The urgent dignity with which she felt and then said the line was an acting lesson in itself.

That moment, and many others like it, contains what I have come to believe is a trademark of Mary Alice's work: In whatever she does, she conveys an astonishing emotional complexity. Whether it be as the title character in Cassandra Medley's *Ma Rose*, part of the Ensemble Studio Theatre's yearly one-act play festival, or as the feisty, no-nonsense Dr. Bessie Delany in Emily Mann's adaptation of the Delany sisters' book *Having Our Say*, her emotional connection to the character is thrilling because it is so dense and multi-layered.

I will never forget Ms. Alice's palpable fury reverberating through Central Park when, in the summer of 1990, she played Queen Margaret prophesying horrible things to come for the House of York and spewing forth her fury at the hunchbacked Duke of Gloucester in Shakespeare's *Richard III*: "Urge neither charity nor shame to me," she said.

> Uncharitably with me have you dealt,
> And shamefully my hopes by you are butcher'd.
> My charity is outrage, life my shame,—
> And in that shame still live my sorrow's rage!

The key to Mary Alice's great emotional accessibility is described, in her own words, candidly and humorously and with great affection for a career in the theatre—a career, by the way, that happened almost by accident.

"All the Parts of Myself Come Together"

I got involved in theatre with no awareness or conscious decision that I wanted to do it professionally. In fact, I was teaching school in Chicago and became involved in theatre as a hobby. During that time I did a show with Douglas Turner Ward, who had come to Chicago with two of his plays, *Day of Absence* and *Happy Ending*. This would have been 1966. He told me he was getting ready to form the Negro Ensemble

Company, and he said that if I ever came to New York and wanted to work, I should look him up.

Shortly after he left, two close friends who were involved in theatre moved to New York. Because I wanted to be with them, I decided that I'd move, too. So I resigned from teaching and came here in July 1967. I called Doug, and he said they were auditioning people for the Negro Ensemble Company. Fortunately, he put me in Lloyd Richards' class. I got my first show in October—two plays by Wole Soyinka called *The Strong Breed* and *The Trials of Brother Jero* at the Greenwich Mews Theatre. But even then I didn't really feel that I wanted to be an actor. I had sort of gotten caught up in acting and hadn't made a conscious decision. A few years after I'd been working in New York, I realized that this was what I wanted to do.

Acting is a kind of exorcism for me. But not really—that's too strong. When I'm acting, it's as if all the parts of myself come together. I feel whole inside when I'm working in theatre, even in rehearsals, but especially during performances. No matter how I'm feeling before—I may be out of kilter, out of sorts—but during the performance, in using myself, I begin to feel whole. Also, acting has helped me know myself more. It's kept me honest.

"I Learned to Use Myself as an Instrument"

Sometimes I use experiences from my own life in acting. I guess most of the time I have. But there are times when I haven't had to, and that's because I've been in an extremely well-written play. I find when the writing's good, I don't have to use my personal experiences as much. The playwright has put so much there to deal with that it takes me along.

My technique as an actress is very affected by classes with Lloyd Richards at the Negro Ensemble Company. The most important thing I learned was how to use myself as an instrument. What I mean is, I learned how to play myself, like a musician, how to be in control of my mind, my body, my voice, my emotions, my imagination. In other words, if I had to, I could stop on a dime in the middle of a performance. If somebody screamed, "Fire," I'd think, "I better get out of here." It doesn't take me much time to come out of character at the end of the performance. When the lights come up for the curtain call, I'm usually still in character, but by the time I get to that dressing room, I'm free.

Lloyd's classes were called "Advanced Acting." We started out with a large group of people, and by the end of that year maybe ten people were left—it was hard work. We worked on scenes, and we worked on monologues. The acting itself is not easy to explain clearly because it's such an intangible process. The most important thing I remember from the class was when Lloyd was critiquing my work he never told me to take anything away. If you needed to change something, he would suggest that you *add* something to it. He'd never say, "Don't do this" or "Don't do that." He'd say, "I want you to start again, and I'd like you to think about this possibility, too." Years later when he was directing me in *Fences*, he did the same thing: He'd suggest that something be added.

Choosing a Role: "I Wasn't Especially Attracted to Rose"
When I'm deciding now if I want to do a role, first of all, I read the play, several times usually. I think about the story, about the characters, about the conflict, if there is any. Then I concentrate on the role that I've been asked to consider. I ask myself: Have I done this role before? How many times have I done it? There are certains kinds of mothers, grandmothers, and other long-suffering women I've played often. If it is similar to a role I've done before, I ask: What about this role makes it different? Is this woman in a slightly different situation? And then, do I think I'm going to want to get up every day and go to rehearsal to work on this character? Is this character interesting enough to me? Does she seem to be complex enough for me to spend the kind of time and energy necessary? And then, do I think I'm going to want to perform this character eight times a week? I also ask, where is this being done? Is it being done in a regional theatre, or is it being done in New York where I can come home every day? I don't do a role just because another actor is going to be in it. Nowadays, fortunately, I don't have to take money into primary consideration. At one time, I had to. And, I go into rehearsal assuming that whoever's directing it knows what he or she's doing. So I base it on those things.

I played Rose Maxson in *Fences*, first, because I had already started the process up at the Eugene O'Neill Center in 1983. The play wasn't in the condition it was in when it finally came to Broadway—it still needed a lot of work. Jimmy [James Earl Jones] wasn't in it, and there was an entirely different cast. It was very long, almost four hours. It was basically the same play, but needed a lot of work. I had no idea that it was going to come to New York. *Ma Rainey's Black Bottom* had been done at the O'Neill but it hadn't come into New York yet. So at that point, *Fences* was just one of many plays.

I wasn't especially attracted to Rose because she was a woman who was too tied to her husband. I know the play dealt with the '50s and things were different then, but the character was too attached to him. I couldn't really see her as an individual. I liked the play, but she wasn't someone who made me feel, "Oh, I'd love to play her." When I was offered the role in the first full production of it at Yale Rep in 1985, I still wasn't too enthusiastic about it. I think the deciding factor was that Lloyd Richards was going to direct it there, and he wanted me to do it. He had always been so wonderful to me. I think a part of me did it just to please him—at least at first. Even though I was a little intimidated at the thought of him directing me—my teacher. I was excited about working with him and Jimmy. But in terms of the role, I wasn't turned on by her.

The way I approached Rose was different from the way I approached any other character—I created Rose as a result of James Earl Jones' character. I realized that the way I felt about working with Jimmy—James Earl Jones, oh boy!!!—was the way Rose felt about Troy. She was in awe of him. She tells her son in the last act how her husband filled the room, he filled up every room he was in. And I just started with the realization—"The feeling I have for Jimmy is the way Rose feels about Troy"—and I created her by reacting to him. It's the only time I've ever done that.

There's a moment in Act III, where she takes the baby and tells him that she'll be the child's mother but that he no longer has a wife. When I was first working on it in rehearsal, I didn't like that line, and I tried to get August to change it. It just seemed old-fashioned to me:

As of right now, this child's got a mother, but you a womanless man.

I didn't want to say it. I can't remember that moment from the O'Neill workshop (maybe it wasn't there). But up at Yale, I said to Lloyd, "That line bothers me," and he discussed it with August, who wanted to keep it. Of course at the first preview, I realized they were absolutely right. When I said it, the house just went crazy. It was one of the most verbal moments in the piece for Rose. Poor Jimmy. He had to stand there by himself after Rose goes inside with the baby. He had to wait by himself until they quieted down. It wasn't his favorite moment.

Once I'd done Rose on stage, I grew to love her, and I think that character would work so beautifully on film, partly because she's so reactive. The story is so dramatic in itself—those huge conflicts within the family. And what happens to Rose is fascinating: She goes to God, brings up the baby girl, but she does maintain Troy's home. The wonderful thing you realize is that she still loves him. When the son comes back, Rose is the one who explains to him why he should love his father. Rose is the one who convinces him to stay for the funeral. In her own way, she's very strong.

Pre-rehearsal Work: "Always Have a Secret"

Once I know I'm going to do a role, there are various things I do to prepare. First, I read the play many times. I make a list of everything the character says about herself and everything that the other characters say about her. I don't question whether it's true or false. I just take it as a given, and I say, "These are all possibilities." They may be true. If another character says, "She's a liar," or, "She cries easily," or "She's unfair," it goes on the list. Whatever is said or suggested about her, I take as a given. I start thinking of this person possibly having all of these attributes.

The other thing I do is break the script down into small units. Sometimes it's a word; sometimes it's a phrase. This breaking down helps me begin to understand how the character thinks—what they say and how they say it. It also helps me learn lines.

I start writing a biography of the character, creating from the play but adding things that are not given in the script—in terms of the early background. In other words, where she was born, when she was born, where she grew up, information about her father and mother (if there was a father and mother in the home). If the parents were divorced, if she were an orphan, if she were an only child, her favorite color, the kind of music she likes—all the things that a person is capable of experiencing. I try to make her as complex as I can. Now, this is information that may never be revealed to the audience, but it feeds me as an actor.

The other thing that Lloyd Richards taught me was to always have a secret. These secrets give you a rich inner life. Just like you've got secrets right now, and they're a part of who you are. If you think about that secret, it's going to do something to you. As an actor, it may do what you need to be doing at that moment. But even if it doesn't, it gives you an inner life; it makes you fuller as a human being. I had a secret for Rose. I had a secret for Dr. Bessie. I had a secret for all of them, but I don't ever tell them.

As I work on the role, the basic secret doesn't change, though other secrets may occur. I may discover something completely new, and I'll feel, "Oh, that's what this really is." That can happen in rehearsal, even during performances. But I try to give her as much as I can before I start rehearsal, so when I begin interacting with the other characters, I have something already going on. I don't want to come in empty.

This work is my basis for the character; that's how I create a character. Now if the character is a real person, like Dr. Bessie, I don't have to depend so much on my imagination. I had the Delany sisters' book *Having Our Say* as a beginning point. I had her talking about herself, how she felt, and I had what her sister Sadie said. We also had a few

"Playing someone who's over a hundred years old means that much of the characterization is in the physicalization. I slowed myself down, physically, making sure I was still able to move well enough to do what I had to do on stage. This slowing down took more energy than moving at my own pace."
Photo by T. L. Boston.

Mary Alice as Dr. Bessie Delany
in Having Our Say.

videos of the sisters that were given to us by the producers. So I saw her moving around and heard her voice. With a real person, again, I start with the given: what she has said about herself. Bessie said she was feisty, and her sister said she was very quick to anger, very outspoken. She didn't like white people except for the ones at St. Augustine and the ones in her family. She loved to laugh, she wasn't afraid to die—she was almost lynched, and she stood up there and said, "I'm ready."

I had to find those points in me, and except for one thing, I did. There was one thing she said about herself that I didn't feel. It wasn't really a disagreement; I just didn't feel the same way. Other than that, I was very much like her, and that was very interesting. I was closer to Dr. Bessie than I ever was to Rose. Like Dr. Bessie, I'm single. I've never had children. I've been a professional person—both a teacher and an actor. Unlike Rose, I don't have the experience of a man bringing me a baby and saying, "This is my baby by another woman." So I had to use my imagination, whereas with Dr. Bessie—even though the circumstances are different, emotionally—I didn't have to reach as far for her, except for the physicalization.

Other Actors in Rehearsal

I want actors who know their craft. I love actors who know how to use the stage, know how to move on it, and realize that body language is very important. I love actors who listen well. I love actors I can trust because they're not going to be thrown if I do something a little different. And because I trust them, I let them know that they can go wherever they have to go spontaneously. What I'm saying is, I love actors who understand the process of acting. I find that sometimes I work with people who don't. Actually, many times. Now if I'm working with someone who doesn't, I just make the mental adjustment, and that is "I better watch myself. I've got to be careful because this person doesn't know what he's doing." He's wooden and acts from the neck up. For instance, if you move in some odd or new way, an uncertain actor will say, "Is she going to upstage me like that?" They don't know how to use the space. If you go upstage, they feel you're upstaging them. They don't know yet that it really doesn't matter. They feel that they have to look at you all the time as they speak. Now if you look into somebody's eyes all the time, you can't keep in mind the object that you need to tell the story. Besides, life is not that way.

Because I'm pretty confident as an actor, I've learned to take care of myself and make the adjustments I need to make if I'm working with someone who's less experienced—or someone who's not necessarily *less* experienced. I've worked with actors who've had more experience than I have and still don't know how to act. I know you know what I'm talking about because you've seen a few.

Now, I try not to make a young actor feel self-conscious. I don't really question what they do. I leave that up to the director. I just make the adjustments that I need to make instead of making them feel insecure. If anything, I try to help them, not necessarily talking to them but in terms of what I do. If they've been told to go here and they go there, I'm not going to get upset, I'll just move somewhere else. There's plenty of stage around for everybody.

"I Have to Do This"

Ultimately, I wanted to do *Having Our Say* because of Dr. Bessie and Miss Sadie Delany. But it wasn't an easy decision. First of all, I got a call from my agent saying that Emily Mann, who was doing the adaptation, had called and wanted to know if I would participate in a reading of *Having Our Say*. Camille Cosby had bought the theatrical rights and she and her partner, Judy James, wanted to hear excerpts from the book read aloud. Emily explained that I would read Dr. Bessie and Gloria Foster would read Miss Sadie and then we'd switch. So we went down to Michael Bennett's old studio and read. At the end of it, Emily asked Judy and Camille, "Should we have them switch?" And they said no.

I realized from the first reading that this was going to be a lot of work. A two-character piece. Two wonderful, complex women, but there's no conflict between them. This is really a performance piece, I thought. What should I do? I don't know. I felt it was one thing to do it at the McCarter Theatre for that limited time period, but another to do it on Broadway. Who knows? It may be a big hit, and that means a long run. So I had to really search my heart. I knew it would be physically demanding, also mentally. But I kept thinking about those two women, and I said, "I have to do this. They're worth it."

Having Our Say: *The Rehearsal Process*
The rehearsal process for *Having Our Say* was difficult. Gloria and I used to walk home and we'd ask, "What is this going to be?" It was hard to learn the lines because there's really no dialogue. I don't think Emily knew when we started what this would ultimately be, but she trusted our instincts. She knew what she wanted physically—the set, the costumes, the projections, the preparation of the meal, etc., but it wasn't until Gloria and I started to work that it began to become clear.

Gloria was incredible in that process in terms of her contribution. In the beginning, we had to find the form for this thing, and that included "discovering" the activities. Emily would say, "By the time you say this, I'd like you to be over at the sink washing the potatoes." But I had to find *how* to get there, a way that was natural for me. I worked moment-to-moment in the beginning, trying to figure it all out. If the director says, "Now, Mary Alice, by the time you pick up the chicken, I want you to be at the sink," I can't just walk there. I have to find a reason for getting up—I have to find the thought that gives me the idea to move. So that while I'm talking and before saying the next line, the thought is already there. I don't want any move to be arbitrary. Another problem: There was no fourth wall. It had been a while since I had done a piece directed at the audience, even though the audience represented one person, our guest for the evening, Amy Hill Hearth.

What makes talking directly to the audience difficult is that you become self-conscious. We were talking to one person, our guest, and yet the guest was all over because it was the whole audience. At first, Emily suggested we speak out directly to where she was sitting. I tried doing that, and I felt it probably wasn't going to work, because if I got into that habit, by the time we were in the theatre, that's where I'd be looking. I knew it would be difficult making the adjustment to open up to the whole audience. And, as you know, I'm sure, the McCarter is an awfully large theatre—it was a big adjustment.

The Physicalization of Old Age

Playing someone who's over a hundred years old means that much of the characterization is in the physicalization. I slowed myself down, physically, making sure I was still able to move well enough to do what I had to do on stage. This slowing down took more energy than moving at my own pace. Reaching for a glass of water or for a cup—everything had to be slowed down to create this illusion that I was 101 years old. Now, we had been told that even though they were over a hundred years old, they were still practicing yoga. They were still doing everything for themselves. Dr. Bessie was still working in the garden, cleaning the furnace. Miss Sadie was doing all the cooking.

For about three days, we sat at the table, reading and discussing. As soon as we got up to start blocking, I started to find that movement. I knew I didn't have to worry about the voice because I had heard Dr. Bessie's voice, and it was very strong, deep, much deeper than mine—surprising for such a small woman.

I never have trouble with lines, but it took me longer to retain the lines because there was no real dialogue, and there was no conflict. I was trying to coordinate that movement—taking food out of the refrigerator, cutting up the carrots—and making sure it was not my rhythm but a rhythm that was believable and consistent with a 101-year-old "feisty." woman. It was the most demanding role I've ever done—not only during the rehearsal process, but the performances as well.

I used my father and my mother in that piece. The walk I found for Dr. Bessie was inspired by my father. But her feistiness, integrity, her committment—she would follow through on something she felt strongly about no matter what—a lot of that was my mother. Some people might call that being stubborn—I think at one point Miss Sadie refers to Dr. Bessie as being stubborn—but she felt things so deeply and strongly. A lot of that was me, but I think I got those qualities from my mother.

"We Had a Connection"

About three days after we finishd the run at Princeton, we met the Delany sisters. We went up to their home. Gloria and I were so excited. When we got there, they were seated at their dining room table. I looked at Dr. Bessie, and she looked at me. We sat around the table and talked. We signed a poster for them, and they signed our books for us. Mrs. Cosby's professional photographer was there and took lots of pictures. We moved to the living room, and they sat in their chairs, which were very much like the chairs in the show. During one of the breaks, Dr. Bessie and I started laughing, and we were the only two people laughing. I knew then we had a connection. When we were leaving, I knelt down in front of her, she took my face in her hands and said, "God bless you," and kissed my forehead.

Meeting her made me feel more secure. Perhaps I could capture her essence. But it wasn't until she actually came to see the show that I knew for sure. We didn't know they were there, fortunately, until the curtain call. At the reception afterwards, I went over to her, knelt beside her, and she said, "I couldn't have done it any better myself." That's when I knew. Amy Hearth told me later that she called me "her actress," and said, "Oh, my actress is just like me." And I believe that basically my spirit is like hers—outspoken, quick to anger, a great sense of humor, and a passionate reaction to injustice.

The Costume Becomes an Integral Part of Who the Character Is

I'm always affected by the costumes I wear. The fact that the blue blouse I wore in *Having Our Say* was Dr. Bessie's favorite color affected me so much. Judy Dearing, our costume designer, told me that she had found a suit with a pattern very much like one Dr. Bessie had. It was a very long skirt, pleated, with a jacket. There was some behavior I came up with for Dr. Bessie because of the costume. I was always pulling the suit forward, smoothing it, putting it into place. As a dentist, she would have a clinical mind. Her thought process was, in some ways, very clinical. I thought that kind of reasoning was with her all the time. When she was seated, I would pull the jacket over. After a while, the costume became an integral part of who the character was for me. When I put on that suit and those shoes, the walk I'd developed for Dr. Bessie would just begin. And the shoes: I have small legs and small ankles, and I wore these big shoes. Sometimes I'd look down at those shoes and think, "Minnie Mouse."

Sometimes I've had a costume that didn't really work and I'd try to justify it, in some way. But I find that costumes, unless they're really costumes like in Shakespeare, are usually not a big problem.

Playing Shakespeare

I approached Queen Margaret in Shakespeare's *Richard III* pretty much the same way I approached Rose in *Fences*. I must say that in terms of approaching Shakespeare, I'm not as comfortable. I've only done three Shakespearean plays. I think I suffer from what many American actors suffer from: feeling intimidated by Shakespeare, not being sure exactly what the language means, the rhythm, and the rhyme. Doing Queen Margaret was the first time I really enjoyed doing Shakespeare, and that was because of the director, Robin Phillips. I really liked him because he trusted me and the cast.

The first time I did Shakespeare I played Cordelia in *King Lear* (Frank Silvera), a production at Arena Stage directed by Ed Sherin. I was so fearful. It was 1968, really the beginning of my career. Ten years later I did Portia in *Julius Caesar*, for the Shakespeare Festival. It was directed by Michael Langham. He was kind of uptight about it, and he didn't feel relaxed working with this group of actors. The company was primarily black and Hispanic, and he just wasn't comfortable. As a result, I don't think the company was comfortable working with him. He tried to get out of it but Mr. Papp wouldn't let him. Consequently, it was not a great experience.

By the time I did *Richard III*, I had a lot more acting experience, and Robin was so sweet. He didn't hold Shakespeare up as some "holy thing." He was casual and loose. He allowed the company to go with it and trusted that the play would work—well, it's worked for more than three hundred years, after all. His feeling was, let's see what we can find with this group of people. He was very lovely, and that experience I really enjoyed.

Maintaining a Performance

When you know you're going to do a role for six months or more, eight times a week, keeping it fresh is very important. The technique for doing that I learned from Lloyd Richards, too: You keep adding to it, either mentally or physically, or both. You keep discovering the way you say a line, or you discover something new in the line itself. To keep it fresh, you have to change it. The character continues growing. The character is never completed.

I tell you, the most meaningful performances for me as an actor are the last couple of weeks. You're on the countdown. There's this nostalgia happening—"Only five more times to pick up this book"—and somehow or other, there's a deepening of everything. You start letting go, but as you let go, it becomes more precious to you. By the last performance you're feeling, "I'm ready to do this role now. I understand who she is."

Approaching a Role in Another Medium

When I create a role for film or television, I go about it differently. I've really done more television than film, but it's basically the same in both, although in the movies you usually have more time. The experience in terms of creating a character is very different because it's so technical. I had to learn to hit my mark. I had to learn that the closer the camera is, the less you have to do. I had to learn to speak softer because there's a boom or a body mike. I had to learn about continuity. It was different and at first felt restrictive. But the biggest adjustment was being in front of a camera instead of an audience.

Now, in terms of the basic work of creating a character, the thought process is the same. I still break my script down into small units; I still create a biography. I still make a list of everything said about me. And, of course, I add a lot of things.

In the late '70s I did a film called *Sparkle*, and that was the first time my character was throughout the film. Mostly I'd worked in movies where I'd had only one or two scenes. So I did something with this one that I'd never done in the theatre: I created my character by myself. This was before the director said anything to me. I laid out my character in terms of where she was emotionally, mentally, physically, one scene to the next, and what happened in between those scenes. I knew where she was supposed to be. Then when the director said, "We're going to do such and such a scene," I'd look at what I'd done and say to myself, "All of this has happened and all of this will happen later, so this scene has got to make sense for her to get from 'here' to 'there.'"

The director didn't know I was doing this—how could he? When we started shooting and he had other ideas, I'd incorporate what he wanted. I'd come home at night and look at what I'd done—I'd add things and take things away according to how he had shot the scene, how that particular scene had actually happened, and then make the adjustments in the scenes that had not been shot. There were, of course, discoveries along the way. But I actually created my basic character on paper.

My best film experience was Phillip Hayes Dean's *The Sty of the Blind Pig*—the role of Alberta Warren. It's the best role I've ever played—actually, I think it's the best role ever written for a black actress. I've never done it on stage. It was first done at the Negro Ensemble Company in 1970–1971 with Frances Foster. When it was done for Hollywood Television Theatre, Phillip requested me after Cicely Tyson—thank God!—turned it down.

This woman was very much like Alma Winemiller in Tennessee Williams' *Summer and Smoke*. In fact, one of the critics compared Alberta to Alma. After we had finished shooting, Phillip asked me once, "How did you know she had a doppelganger?" I said, "It's in the script." Phillip had written a most complex woman. She had these abrupt changes in personality. She lived with her mother and was going through menopause. She went to the doctor every Saturday. She drank. Whenever anyone died, she was called upon to read the eulogy and the telegrams. She made paper flowers, she had no friends, her father had left when she was a baby. She was very nervous and dominated by her mother. Sure enough, at the end of the play, she's trapped in this house—her mother's house—her mother's dead and she's all alone. It's a very sad piece. It was my best film or television experience. It was so close to theatre. We rehearsed for three weeks, like a play, and we shot it in one week, in sequence, from beginning to end.

"A Certain Amount of Mystery"

When I did the weekly televison series, A Different World, I approached the character of Lettie Bostic a little differently. It was a welcome experience for me after Fences. My mother and father had both died during the year I did Fences (1987), and I had been in the hospital in September. So when this offer came, I really wanted to do it because I needed a change.

As soon as I got to California, I felt renewed. I loved Lettie because she was so different from the women I'd been playing: She was very bohemian and a little mysterious. I got to wear great clothes, makeup, nice shoes, and fingernail polish. I worked Monday through Friday. I was off on the weekend—it was so civilized. The first eight shows I liked, but when I returned after the hiatus, the character changed. The director didn't like her wearing a snood and being very bohemian; in other words, she became less interesting and had less to do as the season went on. When I wasn't asked to return for the third season, although I missed all that money, I was relieved and felt liberated.

I accepted the role on the series I'll Fly Away because I wanted to work with Regina Taylor. I had done two of her one-act plays at the Public Theatre. She and the producer Ian Sander wanted me on the show. I had been offered one or two roles before that hadn't interested me. But when I was offered this fascinating woman, Marguerite Peck, I had to do it. She was a single woman, dealing with a certain kind of independence, during a time in the '50s when there was not much offered to black women, certainly not to a black woman who had very little education.

Marguerite could very well have been a maid like Lily, but she made another choice. She was creative, inventive. She was able to adapt. If she thought about going into cosmetology, her attitude was "Okay, I'll go to school for that. And if I want to make hats, I'll learn how to make hats." I thought of her as a traveling saleswoman, even though she really wasn't. It was very fascinating coming up with her background. She had a certain amount of mystery, which was also appealing—a single woman traveling around like that. I found her so very interesting.

BROADWAY

Having Our Say, written and directed by Emily Mann (Tony nomination, Best Actress); *The Shadow Box* by Michael Cristofer; *Fences* by August Wilson, directed by Lloyd Richards (Tony and Drama Desk Awards, Best Featured Actress); *No Place to Be Somebody* by Charles Gordone.

OFF-BROADWAY

Richard III by William Shakespeare, directed by Robin Phillips; *Nongogo* (Obie Award); *Julius Caesar* (Obie Award), *Zooman and the Sign*, *Requiem for a Nun*, *The Trials of Brother Jero*, *The Strong Breed* by Wole Soyinka; *Miss Julie, House Party, Heaven and Hell's Agreement, In the Deepest Part of Sleep, Glasshouse, Ma Rose*.

REGIONAL

The Amen Corner, A Raisin in the Sun, Open Admissions, Gospel at Colonus, Understatements, Take Me Along, For Colored Girls Who Have Considered Suicide When the Rainbow Is Enuf.

FILM

A Perfect World, To Sleep with Anger, On Board, Malcolm X, Life with Mikey, Bonfire of the Vanities, Awakenings, Beat Street, Teachers, Sparkle, The Education of Sonny Carson.

TELEVISION

I'll Fly Away (Emmy Award, Outstanding Guest Performance in a Dramatic Series); *Law & Order, Shelton Avenue, The Resurrection of Lady Lester, The Color of Friendship, A Different World* (Series), *All My Children* (recurring role), *Just an Old Sweet Song, This Man Stands Alone, Requiem for a Nun, The Killing Floor, Concealed Enemies, The Sty of the Blind Pig*.

"I hated my costume for Substance of Fire *with a passion. It was like* Little House on the Prairie. *I don't disagree with Jess Goldstein's intentions—he was following what the play called for. And it worked because it made me feel exactly like Sarah Geldhart feels."*

with Ron Rifkin as her father in *The Substance of Fire*

Sarah Jessica Parker
Substance and Style

I am as familiar with Sarah Jessica Parker's way of working in re-hearsal as I am with anyone else in this book. We have worked to-gether four times, and each one, for me, was a fascinating look at a young actress' growth, both as a performer and as a human being. I stage-managed the original Playwrights Horizons' production of Wendy Wasserstein's *The Heidi Chronicles* in which Sarah Jessica created the roles of Becky (the uncertain, beset teenager in the rap group) and Denise (the on-her-way-to-the-top, ferocious go-getter who's the sister-in-law of that other go-getter, Scoop Rosenbaum). I stage-managed the original production (and its transfer six months later to the Newhouse Theater at Lincoln Center) of Jon Robin Baitz's *The Substance of Fire*, in which Sarah Jessica played the tor-mented, eager-to-please daughter of Isaac Geldhart. Most recently, we worked together on the world premiere of A.R. Gurney's *Sylvia*, in which Sarah Jessica completely captured the hearts of the critics and the public playing a feisty, street-savvy canine who unalterably disrupts the household of Charles Kimbrough and Blythe Danner. Her delightful, and finally touching, performance (which she was performing at the time of our interview) brought her a Drama Desk nomination for best actress, amidst such formidable competition as Zoe Caldwell, Uta Hagen, and Rosemary Harris.

While accomplishing all of the above in theatre—in only six

years—Sarah Jessica has had a quite busy and rather remarkable film career. Her breakthrough role was SanDeE* (yes, that's the spelling), the beautiful and delightfully dim Valley Girl in Steve Martin's charming 1991 comedy, *L.A. Story*. Her performance as SanDeE* made film critics all over the country ecstatic in their praise of her comic skills, as did later film performances as Nicolas Cage's nearly-lost-to-James-Caan girlfriend in *Honeymoon in Vegas*, Johnny Depp's selfish angora-sweater-wearing girlfriend in *Ed Wood*, and her sweetly sardonic turn as Gwyn Marcus in *Miami Rhapsody*. In 1996 alone, she appeared in five films, including *If Lucy Fell*, *Extreme Measures*, and *Mars Attacks!*, and the two that showed to best advantage the subtlety of her range—the gold digger with a heart of stone who steals Bette Midler's husband in *The First Wives Club* and her re-creation of the anxious, skittish Sarah Geldhart in the film version of *The Substance of Fire*.

Watching Sarah Jessica in rehearsal is fascinating. She doesn't seem to do very much for a while. She's definitely prepared; she's done her homework; and in rehearsal she's investigating the scene she's working on—but not a lot happens overtly. A person unacquainted with theatre and the acting process would likely feel that *nothing* is happening. But Sarah Jessica is slowly and carefully putting the elements of the character together, and responding to what she's given by other actors. I remember an early rehearsal of the original New York production of *The Substance of Fire*. Sarah Jessica and Jon Tenney (playing her brother Aaron) were rehearsing a difficult scene. Under director Dan Sullivan's watchful eye, Jon was working on a line that was particularly important because it conveyed both character and plot. He tried it various ways, and each time Sarah Jessica's response was different: a new emphasis on a word in her line, a slight change in body posture, a quick look away as if she were worried someone might be approaching. "I am almost entirely about listening and reacting," she says of her method. That's certainly true, and it's proven by the spontaneity of her performances.

Reviewing her most recent New York performance as Winnifred the Woebegone in the 1996 revival of *Once Upon a Mattress* (about a year after this interview), a major New York critic said, "Sarah Jessica Parker lights up a Broadway stage." Anyone who's ever seen her would agree that her luminous, enchanting presence lights up any stage. It delights me to no end to know that her solid foundation in acting technique will allow her incandescent presence to flourish for many years to come.

The Text, the People, and the Part

When I'm deciding whether I should do a show, the first thing—often before the role itself—is, who am I working with? If the role is small and very good—in the instance of *The Heidi Chronicles*, where I knew I was going to be working with Wendy Wasserstein and André Bishop and Joan Allen—my feeling is, "I'll be there." In terms of theatre, it's what actors are involved, who's directing it, what is the role, and what can I contribute to it.

In terms of the role, I'm more scrutinizing about theatre than I am about film. I will take a bigger risk on stage than on film, but I also want to know that I'm going to be surrounded by Blythe Danner, or Joan Allen, or Ron Rifkin. Being surrounded by good people means there's a standard they will have that I will have to assume. It forces a challenge. In lesser situations, I think I'd be more inclined to be lazy. When I'm under the direction of Dan Sullivan, I'm going to try to step up to the plate every single day. I know that he's going to surround himself with the very best. So it's really those three ingredients: the text, the people, and the part.

A very important thing to me is to never do anything twice. After *L.A. Story*, it would have been very easy, and also very lucrative, for me to do other roles like SanDeE*. I had figured out how to play that character. But to do it over again is just not interesting. There's no risk. And as scary as the risk is, it feeds you and makes you thrive. That role was really important—no one had ever let me play the attractive girl, ever! No one had ever considered me to play a bimbo—I was always the cerebral one, or the best friend of the pretty girl. I loved the role and loved working with Steve Martin.

I wanted to do Sylvia for several reasons. First of all, it was hysterically funny. When I read it to Matthew [Broderick] before the initial reading a year ago, he was laughing out loud, you know, gut laughing, and he said, "You have to do this." That opportunity—playing a dog—had never been presented to me, and probably never will again. How often do they anthropomorphize animals for the theatre? I loved it immediately. She has so many colors. It's an amazing role. Very few roles offer that many emotional opportunities.

My reasons for wanting to play Sarah Geldhart were somewhat different. I wanted to work with Robbie Baitz, and I wanted to work with Dan Sullivan again (he'd directed me in *The Heidi Chronicles* a few years before). When I initially read *The Substance of Fire*, I loved the play. Sarah Geldhart doesn't jump out at you. I found that she was the hardest theatrical role I had to play up to that point because it's always hard to play both sides of the fence, which Sarah does for most of the act. She goes back and forth. There's an intentional flightiness to her that is about her relationship to her father, and Robbie plays that up. And it plagues her. But you can't play that. There's also a wryness to her that's interesting. She's very complicated, but textwise in an uncomplicated way, if you know what I mean.

Approaching a Role: "There Were No Rules in That Room"

I'm very loose in the way I approach a role: I don't consciously look for the intentions, and that's probably a result of having no formal acting training. Now, Blythe Danner does. She says to me almost every night in the dressing room, "I really tried to have a specific intention or objective before the scene." I'm not sure it would work for me, though. I am a totally instinctual person. I don't want to suggest that a person shouldn't study. It serves some people well to have certain kinds of training. For me, though, I am almost entirely about listening and reacting. Now, if I had to sit down and do it, I could find the intentions, absolutely. But to do that—and make it so conscious—would be almost like having too much information in my head. Like a lot of actors, I have limited concentration. I jump from here to there, and have the concentration of a child. I get bored incredibly quickly. So to try to be that focused about the intention of every moment—What do I want? What do I need?—doesn't really help me.

With *Sylvia* though, I was more specific than with any other role I've played. Take the late night scene where Greg, her new master, takes Sylvia walking on the street. He's desperately trying to tell her what's on his mind. She had to listen and not listen. Joey Tillinger kept saying in rehearsal, "We have to be very specific here with the behavior," and he was absolutely right. When I was just naked out there, arbitrarily moving from A to B, it was difficult. The minute it got specific, it felt more comfortable. So there are times when knowing the intentions is applicable, but it's not my first instinct.

Really all I do before rehearsals begin is start reading the script. I don't think a lot about it, because I don't want to plan anything ahead of time. The greatest joy for me is working with people who are different every night. I love it. In the instance of *Sylvia*—because we had that short rehearsal period before going into the theatre—I did read it a lot and began to get familiar with the words. I wanted to liberate myself from the text early in rehearsal.

Mostly, I just go the first day with nothing in mind. I mean, you have a sense of character if the text is good, and that helps enormously. It's a huge first step. When we get into daily rehearsals, I'll try to think about the next day's scene because I know time is now of the essence, and because my concentration is such that I can forget things. I really need to go over my lines very carefully. I'll try to think about what Joey, or whoever the director may be, has said that day and write down questions that I have for him.

From other actors, I'm looking for collaboration and not locking things in too quickly. Experimenting but not to the point of improv—which I really can't stand. It's a waste of time and no one's good at it—well, maybe five people are. I'm looking for people to not be selfish so we can figure things out together. *Sylvia* was a good rehearsal situation for me because nobody wanted to pin things down too quickly. Blythe, up until we left the rehearsal space to begin tech rehearsals, was trying new things in every scene. I was locked in earlier than she because of the unusual nature of the role. There were no rules in that room, which was great.

Approaching a Character in Film

Now with film, I like to do a lot more preparation because you really don't have the rehearsal time to discover things. I want to know more going into it than I would if it were a play. When I played Gwyn Marcus in the film *Miami Rhapsody*, I think we had four or five days of rehearsal. I came to that immediately off of filming *Ed Wood*. (Literally I wrapped *Ed Wood* on Tuesday and flew to Miami on Wednesday. The next day we started work.) I had done very little conscious work—almost nothing—and I was worried. My big concern with the role was that Gwyn was very tough, and so it was necessary to make her sympathetic, too. She had all those one-liners, she's always making jokes. And I wanted to find a way to have her be as witty, smart, and verbally assertive as she was, while having that seem to come from a full person.

Gwyn had such an interesting journey. To me, she was the man in the movie. She was ambivalent about marriage and commitment. In fact, it was a dirty word to her. She was unsure of her own abilities in a monogamous relationship. She was asking all the questions that the man usually asks, and in this movie the man was the girlfriend. She was difficult to get along with—she sabotaged that relationship and then was shocked it was over. And I loved all that and really wanted to play it. I knew, too, it was a good opportunity for me to carry a movie.

I loved the director, David Frankel. Because he was a first-time director, I got to be more involved. My opinion was asked a lot. And the one time we met to discuss the role before filming, I suggested to David that Gwyn's father have some of these one-liners so that you see where it comes from. I didn't want it to look arbitrary that she was the witty, smart one. For instance, there's a scene in the car. I'm riding along with my brother. He's told me that his wife won't sleep with him and he needs a lot of sex. He's just said that he's having an affair with his business partner's wife, and I say to him, "You're like a nuclear menace. You should have your warhead dismantled." It's a very funny line, but I wanted to convey her shock, dismay, and disbelief that he felt that way—to show her humanity, along with her intelligence.

I don't usually do a lot of research. It depends, though. When I played a lawyer, for instance, on the television series, *Equal Justice*, I spent a lot of time at the L.A. County Courthouse. You have to be comfortable playing a particular profession. I spent a lot of time with a woman in the hardcore gang division. She was a young Hispanic woman, and I followed her around. It was helpful just to see what she kept in her office drawer, how she dressed, how she behaved as a woman, how she behaved as an Hispanic, how she behaved with the men in her unit, and helpful to see what she dealt with: It's a revolving door of kids. That division takes care of all gang-related activity in L.A. County, which is about sixty thousand gang members. Someone is a victim one week, and they're the defendant the next.

For *L.A. Story*, I went down to Venice and looked around at the neighborhood that SanDeE* was supposed to be from. But that character is so specific that I couldn't find anyone just like her on the beach. So I do research sometimes if it's a specific thing. But I don't do it to copy or to mimic, just to encourage my imagination.

"I Work Pretty Much the Same Way"

Actually, I approached Sylvia, even though she's a dog, pretty much the same way I approached Sarah in *The Substance of Fire* and Becky and Denise in *The Heidi Chronicles*. There was a different rehearsal atmosphere for *Sylvia* than there was for *Substance* or *Heidi*. The interesting thing about Dan Sullivan as a director is that as hard as you work—and he gets a lot of work done—he's still not strict and scary. But Joey Tillinger, as you know, is so relaxed. Both are great to work with, but their techniques make for a different kind of pressure. Clearly, I attack each role differently because they're different, but I work pretty much the same way.

So I don't need to work on things differently but I certainly need to *think* differently. For instance, the last thing I do before I go on stage every night as Sylvia—as the kids on the crew are pulling the window units on stage in the dark—I go like this [demonstrates her Sylvia posture]—and I'm ready. Another thing I do, in Act II, I'm stage right ready to make my entrance after I've been spayed. As the lights come up on the scene, I drop into what the crew calls the "gutted turkey" position, shoulders hunched and legs spread in that uncomfortable way. That just happens now. I don't think about it. Also, there's something else I do. Every time I have to enter and be running, I can't just run on. I literally have to do this [demonstrates]—I guess you can't write that. It's sort of a take-off. A better way of putting it—a "lift-off." A little leap. There's a ballet word for it—I can't remember it, though I should after all my training. Even when I run off stage to get the ball after Greg has thrown it, I can't re-enter without doing that lift. I've thought, "The crew must think I'm psychotic."

Now, with Sarah Geldhart in *Substance of Fire*, when Patrick Breen as my brother Martin and I were waiting backstage for the top of Act I, in order to get myself tense and excited and out-of-breath, I had to do little relévès. I guess it was because when we entered that boardroom the tension was already high, and I was coming into that meeting with a load of problems. It's not any kind of great trick, but it's my little preparation for the scene.

I've been told by a number of people that in playing Sylvia there's a great deal of "style" in what I'm doing. That's the word that was used—that it's a "stylized" performance. But really what I'm aware of is that, as Sylvia, I have about nine different voices. She's got different voices for every person she has to deal with. It's her way of manipulating people. When Greg first brings her home from the park, she starts off sounding young and sweet. His wife Kate comes on, and she's still young. Greg leaves the stage and she tries to sweet-talk Kate, and when that doesn't work, she turns sassy and there's a different tone of voice—totally different. It drops about an octave. When Greg comes back, she's young again. Then by the end of the act, she's imitating Kate's drunkenness. So I'm not aware of "style," but I'm aware that she's a bit schizophrenic—she's got about nine personalities. If you consider, though, that I'm a woman playing a dog, doing movements that aren't human, I guess it would have to be somewhat stylized.

How Can a Woman Become a Dog?

Rehearsing *Sylvia*, looking for the right way to do "dog" behavior, was so interesting. Joey helped me so much. He has two dogs, Cleo and Menina, and he does wonderful imitations of them. He was constantly showing me Menina's behavior. He's a very good mimic. I didn't want to do Menina, though. She's very different from Sylvia. She's much more prissy. I keep thinking of Menina as one of the Queen's lap dogs, but maybe that's because of Joey's British accent. She's fussy and done. Sylvia's not; she's a street dog. But the physical stuff he gave me was really good. Also, Matthew helped me, though he doesn't realize

*"That opportunity—
playing a dog—had never
been presented to me. I
loved it immediately. How
often do they
anthropomorphize
animals for the theatre?
She has so many colors. It's
an amazing role. Very few
roles have that many
emotional opportunities."*
Photo by Joan Marcus.

*Sarah Jessica Parker with Charles Kimbrough
in* Sylvia.

it. First, because of his border collie, Sally. So many things I do as
Sylvia are based on Sally. Along with Pete Gurney's words, she's my
muse. Every time I sniff one of the cookies, that's exactly how Sally
does it. It's very gentle, she gets as close as she can without touching it,
whereas many dogs would just go for it. But Matthew himself makes
certain faces that I thought were great for Sylvia. I mean, Matthew in
his own life, as well as Matthew playing J. Pierrepont Finch on stage in
How to Succeed. Friends who have now seen his show say, "Are you
aware that you're doing some of what he does?" Two of my friends said
to each other while watching *Sylvia*, "She's doing Matthew."

Also, I use my brother Toby in some of Sylvia's behavior. One specific
place is how I sound when I say, "I feel like a gutted turkey." That's
Toby talking in life. He'll say, "I'm so mad," and he's kind of kidding
but he's kind of serious. I also do the Cowardly Lion, Bert Lahr, when I
say to Kate, "I've sat on couches, I've sat on plenty of couches," and I
learned that from Toby. Now, in terms of technique, the first time I

said, "I've sat on couches," it just came out one day and I thought, "Well, that's the Cowardly Lion," and it grew from there. It's obviously gotten bigger and more sure of itself.

The Director, Specific and General

The director is crucial, of course. He brings his vision, and he makes an atmosphere that's creative. What I look for exactly from the director differs with each project. A lot of times I don't want much help. On *Sylvia*, I really wanted a lot. It was the first time I've wanted that much help. I wanted any idea, tip, clue, direction, advice that Joey Tillinger could come up with. I was desperate for it because I was afraid of this role. I was thrilled to be doing it, but terrified at the potential for disaster, for all of us, but especially for me. Here I was playing a dog. The odds were so stacked against us, especially since I hadn't been on stage for three years, and my movie career had gone in such a direction that had overshadowed my work in theatre. I was afraid that would be taken out on me—"See what happens when someone doesn't continue working in the theatre." "She's just a movie actress now." "See, she doesn't have the chops." But the question was really *how* to do it, and that's what made the rehearsal process for this so fascinating.

We've talked about both Dan Sullivan and Joey Tillinger, and as directors, they're night and day. I felt they both knew what I needed, when I needed it, and how much of it I needed. That's pretty much where the similarity ends. I have always described Dan Sullivan as a surgeon, but it's like new laser surgery. He doesn't cut it all open and make a bloody mess. He goes right to the problem, asks a few simple questions, and it's like a lightbulb goes off for you. Joey, on the other hand, is much more general. He watches, takes notes, and then says, "Well, maybe, you know, how about this?" Dan makes very clean points, though he is not dictatorial. Joey lets you sort of circle around it. They both let you find it. They just have a different attack. Dan's is very specific without being imposing (which is incredibly difficult to do). Joey's is less specific.

I found that Dan was different on *The Substance of Fire* than he was on *The Heidi Chronicles*, which wasn't a communicative experience for me. I didn't know Dan well, and I'm shy around people I don't know well, and he's shy around people he doesn't know well. It was hard to engage him. He had such a reputation that I was really intimidated by him. I remember feeling successful in the roles, but I also remember feeling totally lost during tech rehearsals. I didn't feel comfortable asking him the questions I wanted to ask. Then on *Susbstance of Fire*, I felt there was a settled quality to him. For me, he was just much more porous the second time around, and I knew him better.

I needed much more direction from Dan on *Substance* because finding Sarah Geldhardt was more of an internal search. There wasn't anything Dan or Robbie could have told me. There were many nights, and Robbie will tell you this, that he wasn't happy with my work as Sarah. But there was nothing he could tell me. It was one of those roles you had to find on your own.

It wasn't really until we remounted the show six months later at Lincoln Center that I felt relatively sure of what I was doing. Towards the end of the run at Playwrights, I started to feel that I understood her and I knew I was more in control and equal to the other people on stage. By about the fifth week of performances at Lincoln Center, I started to feel, "This is my role now." But the first few weeks there were still not so good. The women's parts in Robbie's plays are hard. Sarah Geldhart was all over the place; she was incredibly conflicted. It's hard for Robbie to write women that aren't. The course of his men characters is more linear—Aaron, for instance, has a specific thing to play. *Substance of Fire* is really about the men. The two women are there as part of men's lives—it's not their story.

I'm asked a lot if there's been a "best" theatre experience so far. I've had such successful experiences with both Dan and Joey, and they've been entirely different. So it's hard to say. But I'd work with Joey again in a second, and obviously I'd work with Dan. I've done a lot of other plays, but I haven't felt the same way about the experiences.

Costumes on Stage: "It Made Me Feel Exactly like Sarah Geldhart Feels"
I love costumes because they're the exterior that completes the interior life you've been building. When Jane Greenwood put that sweater on me for Sylvia, which is what we were headed toward, it really brought things together. Filthy jeans, clunky shoes, and that big, bulky sweater for the first scene—great costuming. It made me feel, "Yes, this is Sylvia." The outfit Sylvia wears after she's groomed has a different effect—all that fluffy pink, with the pink shoes and pink ribbons. Everyone who's seen the show has mentioned the costumes to me. Well, Jane is fabulous. Depending on what you wear, you stand differently, you walk differently, you talk differently. My walk after the grooming is entirely different from the walk before.

If you're playing a lawyer, for example, the minute you put on heels and stockings, you must carry yourself differently (unless there's a specific reason you don't, and the role calls for you to be uncomfortable). The minute you put a corset on, it changes you. I can almost never wait until dress rehearsal. My feeling is, How soon can I get those clothes on?

I hated my costume for *Substance of Fire* with a passion. I hated the material—all vicose and rayon, not a natural fiber in it—and I hated the way it made me feel. You remember the one I mean, the little white blouse with pink drawstrings and the long print skirt with the high waist. It was like *Little House on the Prairie*. It was perfect for Sarah Geldhart. I don't disagree with this costume for the show. I don't disagree with Jess Goldstein's intentions—he was following what the play called for. And it worked because it made me feel exactly like Sarah Geldhart feels. She's embarrassed to be walking around in lace-up boots and a long skirt. She called herself "a refugee from *Little Women*," and that's just what she looked like. I hated it because I knew she hated it. It's a good thing I had no say on this costume. Had I had my way, I might not have been wearing something that was appropriate.

In the film, one of the scenes will have a similar look, but because it's five years later, that sort of look has changed. It's going to be a flowered dress, I think, but not a skirt and blouse. Also, because there are more scenes that Sarah's in, at different times and places, there will be a variety of looks.

Costumes in Film

In film, it's very different with costumes. I think the costume designer in film is not unlike the writer in theatre, who's present through the entire process. [In film, the writer is mostly not allowed on the set; it's up to the director.] You know, if it's a period piece, as with *Hocus-Pocus*, there's not a lot I can contribute. I don't know about sixteenth-century corsets or whatever. But with contemporary pieces I have a lot of say.

In *Miami Rhapsody*, I chose this odd little blouse with these very long sleeves, and the reason was Gwyn Marcus is a person who doesn't operate from her sexuality, and she's also working in a man's world. She's trying to work up the corporate ladder and is endlessly frustrated. But she's also not someone who shows her figure off. She comes from money, she has expensive, nice things so there's a sense of fashion aesthetic in her choices. But you never see her in a tight dress. Everything I wore was modest, covered, high. And so that blouse covered even the hands. But I wore a lot of big men's khakis and stuff like that.

Patricia Field was the designer, and she was very flexible. When we got more into men's clothing, that was the director David Frankel's idea because his girlfriend dresses like that. My idea at first was to base it on a friend in L.A. who is an executive in a television company. I thought the way she dresses was perfect for this character. We tried it, and David didn't buy it. He liked the more asexual look on this character.

Now, I didn't really know that until about three weeks into the shooting when we'd been changing the outfits every day. We were shooting one night and having a really hard time with the scene, and he said to me, "Her sexuality is all here" [indicating from her neck to the top of her head]. And I said, "Oh, oh, oh." Nothing below the neck—and that made a lot of sense for that character. So I realized what he was after and why the clothes had been changing. This was about halfway through shooting, and then everything was clear and got set.

From Stage to Film

It's interesting that we start rehearsals on Monday for the film of *Substance*. In one sense, it's like riding a bike. It comes back to you. Hopefully, it will come back where my battery had been charged (not where it was depleted), and I'll have the nuances I had found at Lincoln Center. But there's a whole new dimension to Sarah Geldhart now. In the film, she has a relationship with a man outside her relationship with her father and brothers, and we see it—it's not just alluded to, as it was in the play. That relationship is complicated too. I haven't played that aspect of Sarah, so there's a new part of her I don't know at all. It's got to add new colors.

Preparing for shooting the film, I've been thinking about Sarah Geldhart on stage and on camera. You have to be bigger on stage. You can't not be. Nuances are different on stage than they are on screen. You know, on screen you can be so little and the camera catches everything. With theatre, the subtleties are bigger. Subtleties on stage would be like fireworks going off in film. I did Sarah Geldhart in the one-hundred-forty-five-seat theatre at Playwrights Horizons and in the three-hundred-seat Newhouse at Lincoln Center Theater, and now I'll be playing her with the camera very close. There will be some differences, I'm sure. I think I'll have to take things down, and that's easier for me than bringing them up. It's going to have to be quieter. It's a pretty quiet piece anyway. The emotions are enormous—sad, profound, and complex—but it's not a raucous comedy. I think we have to find the temperament for all of us.

Of course, we'll likely shoot out-of-sequence because most all movies are, and it can be very hard. The danger is to play the end of the movie at the beginning. I think in this case we're going to do the funeral near the end of shooting. It's not easy, for instance, when you're in a romantic comedy and you do the love scenes the first week of shooting—and it always happens that way. You don't know the person at all. Six weeks into shooting you think, "God, I wish we could shoot that scene now because we love each other or hate each other," or whatever it's supposed to be.

The only way to make it work when you shoot out-of-sequence is to constantly remind yourself what happened before this, and what's happening after. Often I'll ask the script supervisor, "What went on right before I came here and got out of the cab? Is that before I talked to my father or after I talked to him?" On a movie you have to have a good script supervisor. I am meticulous about that, just as I'm meticulous about props and continuity and before and after each scene. Mostly I've had great script supervisors. When you don't, it sucks—it's really frustrating.

One scary thing when you're shooting a movie is knowing when you're good or not. You can sort of tell. You know when you feel pretty good. What you don't know is when they say you were good and you didn't think you were. That's when you're scared because you have to trust a virtual stranger. You lose perspective, too. Take seven, take nine, take eleven—which was the best? And, you know, often the first take was the best one. Some people have that theory and there's something to be said for it. It's a fresh moment.

Approaching the Role in a TV Series

I don't think I approach understanding the character differently in a series. The great thing about a series is that the character you play leads a whole life. With a play, you only see a certain portion of a person's life. The same is true of a movie. But with a series, you get to experience all these different things in a person's life.

In a weekly television series, working on a role is much easier after a while. It's not unlike working in a factory—not that you take it any the less seriously. You come in every day and you already know the character. You start to think you know it better than the writers and better than any director who's going to direct an episode. You're so comfortable and you're there for so long—meaning so many months a year and hours a day—that it really becomes rote. You start to learn your lines very quickly. You can have nine pages of dialogue the next day and, boom!, you know it.

In that sense it's easy. The hard part is that it's time-consuming and draining. For years I didn't agree with that. When I was on *Square Pegs*, I loved doing it. It was really fun. I would hear adults say, "I'm so burned out. I'm so exhausted." And I felt, "I'm never going to be like that. I've got this great job, working with great people."

By the end of the third series, *Equal Justice*, I was burned out. I'd leave my house at 4:15 in the morning, literally every day from July to February. You're shooting an hour script in a week, or, at most, ten days. I would get home at 9:00 at night, get some food—you never cook at home, you rarely see other people—you get into bed and learn your lines and wake up again at 3:30 in the morning to wash and dry your hair. After two years of that, I was so tired. It's not that you're working the whole time—that would be easier. On the set, you wait. I read, I knitted blankets, etc. It dissipates your energy in a way that's hard to explain. Every night at the end of *Sylvia*, I'm tired but filled with more energy. At the end of a shooting day, you're done in. It's a totally different energy.

Of the three series I did, *A Year in the Life* was the most enjoyable because I was at a point in my career where film opportunities were not so present, and I didn't feel like I was missing out on so much. On my hiatus, I was able to do television movies-of-the-week and come to New York and do plays. But with *Equal Justice*, I began to feel that I was being held back. It was a great show—I had some terrific episodes and it was the most mature role I'd ever had—but I wanted more to do. I was at the point in my career where I was itching to do more. I started to feel tied up and stagnant. I would get a script for the next week and be frustrated because I wanted to be more a part of it. We had ten terrific actors, many of them from New York—Barry Miller, Cotter Smith, Jane Kaczmarek, Joe Morton, Jon Tenney—all dying to do their stuff.

You get very comfortable in a series. You can slip in and out of your character in two seconds. They can say, "Cut," and you can stop for a few minutes, and then go right back to the phone call you're shooting about the devastating death of a cousin. And you're comfortable. You know the crew so well that you might make a joke as the person has the clapper in front of your face, and then you're right in the scene. It's very familial and comfortable. And that's the danger of it, too. That's why people don't want to get out of them.

A Successful Transition

There were several things that contributed to my wanting to act when I was a child. The first real reason was that it got me out of school. I swear to God, that's the truth. I didn't like school. I hated doing school work. Then I did this movie called *The Little Match Girl*, and it was so much fun. They paid me money, and that was great because we didn't have any money. So it was a big deal to have a little money. I was treated as very special, and that's not the treatment I got at home. I wasn't the center of attention there because there were eight of us.

I was eight when I began studying with the Cincinnati Ballet Company, which had a wonderful reputation. That was my first real introduction to expressing myself, and I loved it. While I was studying ballet, I also knew I liked acting. But I thought I was going to be a ballet dancer because it seemed much more doable in Cincinnati. There are only a few opportunities for actors there. I had great teachers who talked a lot about the emotional life of a ballet dancer. And there were women in the ballet company that I really admired, looked up to, and wanted to be like.

An important time was when my family came to New York and saw *A Chorus Line*. I think we saw it a week before it opened on Broadway. This sounds like a really embarrassing cliche, but it spoke to me. And I knew I wanted to do that. I don't know how focused I was, but I knew that this was what would make me happy. My whole family loved musicals. We listened to cast albums of shows all the time. I loved singing and I loved acting.

I didn't actually study voice until I got the role of Annie, and then I studied because we didn't want my voice to get hurt. I had never sung a note in public before doing a Milliken Breakfast Show in New York. Then I did *By Strouse* at Manhattan Theatre Club—that was 1977. I auditioned for *Annie* right after it opened on Broadway. My whole family had gotten standing room to see it, and I wanted to be in it desperately. "I have to be in that show. Those kids are the luckiest kids in America." I didn't get it then, and I went on the road with *The Sound of Music*. After the tour, I became one of the orphans and was Annie's understudy. I couldn't believe how lucky I was.

Now, when I took over the role of Annie, there was not a happier moment in my life. I was very conscious of rehearsal hours, learning lines, being on time to rehearsal, and that was because of my parents. They taught me about the responsibility of that job, and I took it very seriously. I remember being told by my father many times about projection, about not ever "walking through a show." I remember my dad saying to me, "You better be serious about this because it's a big adult responsibility, and you are expected to act like an adult when you're at the show." So I knew I had to project, had to hit my mark every night in certain places. But I also happened to be with a company of people who loved having a good time. They loved doing *Annie*. I knew there were rules that actors had to adhere to; I took them very seriously. I've always been a rule taker.

I played Annie for a year. I think I just assumed then that I would become an actor as my lifetime job because that's all I knew how to do. I stopped ballet when I took over the role of Annie. I knew I wasn't academically inclined. I'm not sure I thought I had much choice. And it wasn't that I thought I was so gifted and had something to offer. I felt like I couldn't do anything else, but I had incredible reverence and respect for it. I had an affinity for other actors. I wanted to be around them. Every member of that chorus was my best friend.

My home life would have been considered very normal, and in that way I was different from the other kids in *Annie*. We'd moved to New York by that time, but my mom didn't come to the theatre at all. I took the subway to and from the theatre every night. These were theatre kids, and I went home to seven brothers and sisters. That may be one of the things that saved me.

I've been very fortunate in that I've made a pretty successful transition from a child actor to an adult actor. I think part of it is, frankly, just luck. I really do. And the other half is wanting the right things. Working in the theatre has helped tremendously, especially in the awkward years. It was helpful to do theatre as opposed to movies and television—where you're exposed to huge numbers and everyone picks on you for being an awkward teenager. And I think wanting a full career—theatre, television, and film—helped. Working with good people, which had been instilled in me early, by my earliest experiences. I'm very particular now about who I work with. As a young person, I didn't want to do trash and big television series just for the money. My parents did not want me to do a television series when I was young. They were even concerned about my doing *Square Pegs*. I think because I had those standards, it saved me from having a career like Macauley Culkin, who's become a commodity. Now what happens to him? It's unfair to the child, because it sets up a structure that can't stay in place.

I care about what I do. I don't ever want to be difficult to work with. And frankly, I'm baffled by those who make it hard on themselves and others. Why can't you show up on time? Why can't you be decent to the people around you? It's simply unprofessional, and blatant shirking of your professional responsibilities is unacceptable to me on any level.

BROADWAY
Once Upon a Mattress, How to Succeed in Business Without Really Trying, Annie (title role), *The Innocents*

OFF-BROADWAY
Sylvia by A.R. Gurney, directed by John Tillinger, costumes designed by Jane Greenwood (Drama Desk Nomination, Best Actress); *The Substance of Fire* by Jon Robin Baitz, directed by Daniel Sullivan, costumes designed by Jess Goldstein; *The Heidi Chronicles, To Gillian on Her 37th Birthday, April Snow, By Strouse.*

FILM

Til There Was You, Mars Attacks!, The First Wives Club, Extreme Measures, The Substance of Fire, If Lucy Fell, Miami Rhapsody, Ed Wood, Striking Distance, Honeymoon in Vegas, Hocus Pocus, L.A. Story, Firstborn.

TELEVISION

Series: *Equal Justice, A Year in the Life, Square Pegs.* Films: Neil Simon's *The Sunshine Boys; My Body, My Child* (with Vanessa Redgrave); *Life Under Water; In the Best Interests of the Children.*

"The costume was wonderful in two ways: It helped me know who Anna was; and it helped me create the way she moved."

as Anna Christie in *New Girl in Town*

Gwen Verdon
Earned Innocence

One of my most vivid memories in theatre-going is seeing Gwen Verdon perform Charity Hope Valentine in the musical comedy, *Sweet Charity*. It was mid-June, 1966. I was in New York for two days of non-stop theatre-going, before continuing on to Connecticut where I was to be assistant props master at the Ivoryton Playhouse, then a summer "star-package" theatre. I got a single, obstructed-view seat (even though it was in the third row of the recently reopened Palace Theatre, I had to watch peering around a rather large pole) for the enormous price of $12.90, an all-time high then for a musical comedy.

I would have paid twice that amount to see Gwen Verdon. Being an avid fan of Broadway musicals from twelve hundred miles away, I had long ago memorized all the lyrics to the original cast recording of *Damn Yankees*, the show that made Miss Verdon a national star. And in the months preceding this trip, I had listened to the recording of *Sweet Charity* so many times that I had almost mastered the lyrics to all of its songs.

I will never forget Miss Verdon's first appearance and the effect it had on the entire audience. Just as the overture ended, the house curtain went up, and a follow spot caught her center stage in the "Charity" pose—purse on a string slung over her left shoulder, right hand on a thrust-out hip, left high-heeled pump tapping in rhythm to the music—a combination (we learn from her interview) of her own creation and the dancing style of Bob Fosse, her husband and the show's director and choreographer. This was my introduction to the full-figure Fosse silhouette, in the form of the person who most helped him define it.

Exuding a unique combination of both innocence and sensuality, Miss Verdon slowly looked over her left shoulder. When she caught sight of us, she smiled, first tentatively, then radiantly acknowledging our presence, and the audience went crazy. She was forced to stand still for several moments while the roar from the house continued and the orchestra vamped. This magical interaction between performer and audience is one of the things that makes live theatre the great experience it is. In 1966, I'd never seen anything quite like it, and—is it necessary to say?—I've never forgotten it. When I asked her how aware she was of this particular kind of effect on an audience over the years of her career, she said, "I know it's there but it surprises me every time."

Gwen Verdon is probably the greatest dancing musical star in Broadway history—four Tony Awards out of six nominations is some evidence for this fact. (The one rival for this title is her friend of over forty years, Chita Rivera. They have appeared together—only once though—in the original production of Kander and Ebb's *Chicago*.) As Miss Verdon discusses her nearly thirty-year reign as a Broadway musical star, we learn about her own technique and how she got to it. But we also get two great bonuses.

First, we're reintroduced to the style of Broadway dancing she and Bob Fosse invented—those quintessential gestures that not every good dancer can bring off: fingers snapping, body boldly strutting, the forwardly thrust pelvis, the shrugging shoulders (sometimes one at a time, sometimes together), the use of hats and canes, of arms and legs as well as hands and feet. A singular style not like any other before.

Second, the discussion of Miss Verdon's career and Mr. Fosse's influence on it resonates with the last forty years (and more, actually) of American musical theatre history. It includes composers Cole Porter, Richard Adler and Jerry Ross, Bob Merrill, Albert Hague and Dorothy Fields, Cy Coleman, John Kander and Fred Ebb; writers Douglas Wallop, Eugene O'Neill, Sidney Sheldon, Neil Simon; directors Abe Burrows and George Abbott; designers Jo Mielziner, Motley, Rouben Ter-Arutunian, William and Jean Eckart, Robert Randolph, Irene Sharaff, Tony Walton, Patricia Zipprodt, and Jules Fisher; and choreographers Jack Cole, Michael

Kidd, and, of course, Bob Fosse, wearing both his hats as director and choreographer.

Gwen Verdon made an indelible mark in American theatrical history, and her career that began over five decades ago continues. She has become a subtle, thoughtful character actress of great depth—often quite funny. A fine instance is her delightful performance as Aunt Ruth in the 1996 film version of Scott McPherson's *Marvin's Room*.

I don't remember exactly when I started dancing. My mother was a dancer, so I thought everybody and their mother danced. In addition to performing, she also taught, so I was always in class—ballet, tap. By the age of two or so, I could do regular splits, front splits, stand on my head. I was a contortionist. My legs, though, were so crooked that my mother took me to the orthopedic hospital in Los Angeles. They explained that the muscles on the inside of the leg were too long for the muscles on the outside. They suggested breaking my legs and resetting them. My mother didn't want to do that so she came up with exercises that would not stretch the inside muscles anymore. Since she danced with Ruth St. Denis, I studied that kind of dancing because you didn't have to turn out or use those particular muscles.

"That I Remember—My First Laugh"

I don't remember when I first performed in public, but I do remember my first time before an audience. In Los Angeles they had a Cotton Club. My mother worked there as a dancer doing ethnic dancing, which was "pseudo" Oriental. The dinner show was all white; the midnight show was all black. Then they closed down, and at 2:00 A.M. there was a mixed show—which was apparently quite unique then. One night, my father (who worked for MGM) piled my brother and me into the car, drove to the Cotton Club, and said to me, "Go get your mother." I was three and a half. I got out of the car (I was in my pajamas), walked up the red carpet that led you right into the club. I was below table level, but to me it looked like a dream world because it was all candle lit. The red carpet led me right up on stage, and there was Willie Covan, a black tap dancer. "Oh," he said, "what can I do for you?" "I want my mother." The audience laughed. *That* I remember—my first laugh, and it's the first time I remember being on stage.

There did come a point when I knew I wanted to become a professional dancer. I had quit dancing when I was fifteen years old because I didn't like the routine or such rigid discipline. And I didn't dance for, I guess, about three years. Then I saw Jack Cole and his group perform in a nightclub. It was a revelation. Light bulbs went off for me. I'd never thought of dancing that way. They did all this East Indian, Afro-Cuban movement, and it had a jazz feel. I'd never seen people move like that. It was so full emotionally. You could see that you needed the technique of ballet and modern, but it had something more. I just loved what they were doing. I went backstage and talked to him. I told him I hadn't danced in three years. He said, "Well, get in condition and we'll see what happens." So I went back to class, got in shape, and auditioned for him at Columbia Studios. I got the job.

I worked with Jack for about seven years. I think I responded to his kind of dance because it seemed to have more character in it than simply ballet or tap. As an actress, as you play the character—temporarily, mind you—you *become* that person. It's a great escape from yourself. Jack's dancing had that kind of escape. I mean, you could be an East Indian doing all this fancy stuff. I became so intrigued that I studied with La Meri and Uday Shankar. Jack knew that I didn't have the most desirable education. So he and his friend David Gray took me under their wing. By this time, we were in Chicago performing at the Chez Paris. I had classes at the nightclub with Jack just before the performance. In the daytime, I was with David learning everything you could learn in museums and libraries. I loved what I was doing so much that I thought, "This sure isn't gonna last," so I took a correspondence course to be a secretary—typing and shorthand.

At this point when I was dancing in the late '40s, I didn't have any idea that I wanted, or might want, to act. But I do think you had to be able to act, really, to do Jack's dancing. When I was a kid, I used to imitate everybody around me. Not performers but schoolteachers, people's parents, other people I met—just for the fun of it. I was doing that when I was with Jack's company. I imitated people, and David kept saying to me, "You should do musical comedy." So I guess a desire to act was around somehow, though not consciously.

Claudine: Can-Can

The first "formal" acting I did was as Claudine in Cole Porter's *Can-Can* in 1953. But really, I'd acted before because in order to be a good dancer you've got to know how to act—to a degree, anyway. I mean, if you have no life and no emotion to express through dance, then you don't dance. I don't care how much you pick 'em up and put 'em down—without emotion, you're not dancing. In Jack Cole's *Alive and Kicking*, we had to act. We played children who spied on a young couple holding hands or kissing. You had to act like a child—which was great fun.

I was assisting Jack on a movie he was choreographing at 20th Century Fox. Michael Kidd, who was choreographing on the next soundstage, asked if I would audition for *Can-Can*. He said, "We'll pay your way, you'll stay in New York for a weekend, and we'll get you back in time for Monday's shoot." I went to New York, and Michael let me do my own dance. I sang "Pennies from Heaven," which has an octave jump in it. (I've never been able to really sing. I can fake it pretty well.) Then I had to do a scene with the stage manager, and it seemed like such a silly scene to me. "You're supposed to be an ingenue," they explained. So I said, "Isn't 'ingenue' something that was back at the turn of the century?" And they said, "Yes, this play takes place at that time." Well, I got the job.

I knew very little about "formal" acting. My mother explained that an ingenue is always the young, unknowing girl in a play or musical, and I thought, "Okay, I'm an ingenue." I had studied acting, but the approach was so old-fashioned. It was how to do falls or how to run to your mother and slide into her. That was the extent of acting with Willie Covan. I had studied mime with Jean-Louis Barrault when I was dancing in Paris with Jack's company. And, like dance, mime is acting without words but body movement— so it was perfect for me at that time.

I had read all of the Claudine books by Colette—that was part of the education that Jack and David Gray gave me. I thought, "She's going to be Colette's Claudine. And she'll have LaGoulue's hair." But really, I approached it, I think, from the dance. And, I'm afraid, I gave Michael Kidd a very hard time. I felt he wasn't giving me enough good things to do, and his choreography was very athletic. It was "Kick here, jump there, cartwheel here, and then split." It was, for me, just jumping around—not emotionally based.

I had come from a completely different dance background. When we got to the Garden of Eden number, I said, "Can I do something that's very much like Ruth St. Denis?" And I did the beginning of a dance where Eve is supposed to be innocent. It was based on a dance my mother had done when she was with Ruth St. Denis. It was that "hell-bent-for-beauty" type dancing—you sort of pointed your foot, but it was really very Isadora Duncan-ish. But, as Claudine, I really didn't know what I was doing.

Lola in Damn Yankees: "The Character Came Out of the Dance"
In 1955, I worked on *Damn Yankees* with George Abbott as director and Bob Fosse the choreographer, and that was the beginning of my learning something that would help me technically as an actress. George didn't believe in any of that. He said, "Say the words and get

off." That's what you're supposed to do, and that's what I began doing. It was pretty simple.

The only research I did for Lola was I spent many hours on Eighth Avenue, observing. It was primarily Cuban at that time, Cuban-Puerto Rican. And very safe. It was all families. The grandmother had a parrot, and the grandchildren had lace on their socks. I could observe the attitude of people, and I learned the Spanish accent—well, a "pseudo" Spanish accent for Lola.

I always felt that Lola was a child. You know, everyone said to me that it was so sexy. I didn't think it was sexy. I did think she was funny. When I thought of Lola, I was reminded of Lola Montez, and all those movie ladies of the '30s and '40s, who, when they had to be sexy, had flaring nostrils and eye attitude. They looked funny to me. They were my models for Lola. But I didn't act like it was funny. I just did it, and *meant* every word.

The first thing I learned for the show was the "Whatever Lola Wants" number. Bob taught me that dance first—both the song and the dance. He was so specific in terms of movement—and there was talking within the dance—that most of the character really came out of that dance. Now Bob always worked to classical music. We did the entire Lola number—all those Billy the Kid vamps—accompanied by recordings of Aaron Copland and Morton Gould. Whenever Bob wanted me to learn a step with a certain oddball phrasing, he would use classical music. He choreographed every single thing in the number, right down to the end: after the dance, the song comes back in, and he directed me to push my hair back—a very specific movement—so it wouldn't be in my face for the rest of the scene. It was very minute and precise.

There were only two scenes in *Damn Yankees* where I actually had to act. Because he had studied acting himself, Bob coached me on them. In the scene where Lola tells Joe that she was the ugliest woman in Providence, Rhode Island, I was just saying the words. Bob saw that they didn't mean enough. "You've got to reveal or tell a secret about yourself," he said. "Think about something you did that you feel sorry for now, something that you still feel guilty about. Keep that in mind, and say those words." So that's what I did. I thought of the times I used to steal things when I was a kid.

But using what happened in my life to fill me for something in a scene was not a way of working I liked. It was too personal. And it worried me; what if you can't remember something one night? Or, what if the memory doesn't return when you need it? You've got to have some kind of technique, and some kind of style that you can call on, just as you do in dance. I mean, as a dancer, if you don't, or can't, get all revved up to perform a certain way, you've got your technique. You may not be brilliant, but you'll be good. That's what technique does.

Anna Christie: New Girl in Town

So I began studying with Sandy Meisner in order to learn some kind of acting technique. We worked on scenes from *New Girl in Town*, a musical version of O'Neill's *Anna Christie* that I did in 1958 after *Damn Yankees*. That was the first time I approached acting from a particular point of view. Studying with Sandy, I had an actor working with me, and we did all the original O'Neill scenes. That was very exciting. Unfortunately, they were eventually almost completely cut from *New Girl*. We'd be doing some of the same dialogue but in a spotlight in preparation for a big tap number. I was very disappointed, and I found it emotionally wearing. I had not discovered yet really how to use the technique.

In order to make it work, I had to take some of the emotional stuff from the scenes into the dancing. Fortunately, Bob said that when Anna dances, she's free because she's proud of the fact that she's been absolutely honest and she hated her life. She's proud, and no one is going to put her down for it. So there was an honesty in the character. But after six months, I hated doing it. I thought, "I don't want to work this way."

Not too long afterward, I read a book by Sir Laurence Olivier. In it, he said that he could never really understand the Actors' Studio method, nor could he understand working on a character from "within," or plumbing up through all your guilt feelings. And I thought, "Oh, I know just how you feel." He explained that he's gone through his career working from the "outside in"—remembering somebody's walk, or a funny little tic they had, or a certain way of holding themselves. He would put on some clothes or use certain props and find out how that affected his behavior and who the character was. I'd say basically that's the way I work.

One of the best-known numbers from *New Girl in Town*, "There Ain't No Flies on Me," is a dance number that shows something about Bob's work. There was the use of straw hats, which later became a trademark of his. He always used hats. He loved props. If you had asked him why, he would have said, "Because I was going bald when I was seventeen." But he loved the specificity of props and what that did to the dancer. He loved precision. First, we didn't just snap our fingers. We snapped them with the hand turned down and the thumb on top. We tucked in our chins tight against our necks. And I remember he asked us to make a saucer with our hands. All of that was very specifically directed.

"The Costume Helped Me Know Who Anna Was"

I'm very much affected by the clothes I wear, and the clothes in *New Girl in Town* were particularly significant. There's a photograph from the show—probably the best-known one—and you can see the arrival outfit that Rouben Ter-Arutunian designed for me. We wanted a satin skirt but felt it was too bright, so we covered it with the black netting. And then we got the corset look. The gloves she wore were made out of mesh stockings, but we put flowers on them. And the ratty fur piece I wore around my neck belonged to the lady who was running the shop, Mrs. Pons. When I saw it, I said, "Oh, that's perfect. It's just the right look." Now, the earrings I wore there have a personal meaning for me. Jack Cole gave them to me on opening night of *Can-Can*, and I wore them in every single show after that.

That costume was wonderful in two ways: It helped me know who Anna was, and it helped me create the way she moved. For instance, the satin dress was so tight it made you walk a certain way, and because that girdle scrunched you in, you had to have a certain upright posture. That whole outfit had a lived-in feel to it and looked absolutely antique because of the net over the satin and that rotten little fur piece. And the hat was perfect—sort of jaunty and drooping at the same time, like Anna herself.

The high point of *New Girl in Town* was doing the first scene, which was original to O'Neill's play. Anna comes in and speaks with Marthy, who was played by Thelma Ritter. The song that Bob Merrill wrote was just fantastic—"On the Farm." Anna sings this to her father. He's so thrilled to see me that he doesn't realize what I'm saying. The tune is charming and lively, but I'm singing things like:

> On the farm, on the farm,
> Country butter, eggs by the dozens,
> Getting grabbed by all my cousins,
> On the farm.

And later:

> In the barn with Uncle Jake,
> If you squeal,
> You get the rake.

And the last line is, "With those vicious sons' of bitches on the farm." It wasn't done with any anger, just level and factual. In fact, Bob gave me a wonderful direction. He said, "Don't move. Just stand there." That's the hardest thing I ever did. You just stand, one hand on the chair, and the other hand just hanging. And in that quiet way, you reveal your whole life.

The most difficult thing about *New Girl* was the way it was changed—we kept losing O'Neill's play. It was sad. In the original, Anna told her father about her former life as a prostitute. In the musical, she tells Mat, and Mat just storms out. Then the dream ballet happened. (Now, that has a history, too. That ballet was cut out because some people felt it was vulgar; then it was changed and put back in after we had opened in New York.) But that scene was difficult for me. I had no idea what it was like to be forced into prostitution. To me, it's the most vile thing, the most degrading thing that can happen to a person. And yet I have sympathy for these women. But playing it was hard because, as I said, I didn't know how yet.

Essie Whimple: Redhead

In 1959 came *Redhead*. I loved that show. It may be my favorite, and I loved playing Essie Whimple, a homely, cockney girl working with her aunts in the wax museum. Essie has learned the identity of a murderer. In order to hide me, I become part of an American traveling circus, where Richard Kiley is a weightlifter.

Bob choreographed some wonderful numbers. When we were working on "'Erbie Fitch's Twitch," I knew I'd have to wear some kind of man's clothing because in the scene I'm imitating my father. Learning that particular number in rehearsal in a pair of tights wasn't very useful. So I borrowed Bob's jacket one day and worked in that for a while, then later added the pants. Putting on that jacket, moving around in it, dancing, jumping about—all helped me find 'Erbie.

Doing 'Erbie was such fun because he was so tomboy and pathetic. I admit I just plain imitated Sir Laurence Olivier as Archie Rice in *The Entertainer*. Olivier and Bob Fosse are really the two people most responsible for any kind of growth of mine as an actress after Jack Cole. Jack and Bob were the two most important men in my life. When I was first working on it, I knew 'Erbie needed to be shabby. I was learning to twirl the cane, and suddenly I got the image of Olivier as Archie Rice, and it just seemed right.

Then I tackled the song. I don't know if you're aware of how much it speeds up. They wanted me to go as fast as Danny Kaye in the "Tchaikovsky" number in *Lady in the Dark*. So I started slowly, saying the words very precisely:

Gwen Verdon in Redhead.

"I can assure you this was all ballet, but you can see from the way the hands are used that it's not typical ballet. You had to have the training, however, to do it." Al Hirschfeld drawing courtesy Margo Feiden Galleries.

'Erbie Fitch is me name,
And I'm in a bit of a pickle,
I must say to me shame I'm fickle.

And then building up a little speed:

I've a bit of a twitch
For a witch
I met in Ipswich.

And then faster:

But the hitch
Is the Ipswich witch
Which is the one I wed.

Finally, my mouth just did it—I worked so hard on it that when I repeated it, I wouldn't have to think about it. It was hard but very satisfying.

"'Erbie Fitch's Twitch" was the first time Bob directed me to talk directly to the audience. It scared me to death, absolutely terrified me to make that eye contact. Then, I'm afraid, later I was such a hambone that I loved it, particularly when I did it in *Chicago*.

I loved doing *Redhead* because once Essie has become part of the traveling show, she's supposed to be a big flop. She's wasn't supposed to be good at performing. All the characters are on stage watching me perform "'Erbie Fitch's Twitch." I'd tell a joke that wasn't funny, and they'd just look at me like I was a bug. I'd apologize and say with the cockney accent, "Me daddy used to say lots of things like that." Learning the cockney wasn't difficult—my whole family is cockney. In fact, I was so adept at it that they said, "Back off from it a bit," because, of course, you'd never understand a real cockney.

The most memorable part of doing *Redhead* was in the beginning of the show. I'm just plain Essie Whimple at the waxworks museum. I wore a brown wig, very severe, sort of a Jane Eyre look. Being the ugly duckling, in love with Richard Kiley, and just swooning over him was so much fun. He'd look at me like, "Ugh, the last woman I'd consider." There's a wonderful innocence about Essie. Innocence is a quality that has sometimes been attributed to me as an actress. I didn't do it deliberately, but somehow or other it seems to come through. In acting class, I used to do scenes from *The Madwoman of Chaillot*, who of course is mad but there's an innocence about her: She puts flowers down the sewer so the sewer man can have a bit of pleasure on the job. To me that makes sense. She's not stupid, she's just, well . . . off center. That innocense is in Charity. It's even in Roxie Hart. Roxie may have murdered her lover, but she felt she was just taking care of herself.

Redhead was the third collaboration with Bob. I grew as both an actress and a dancer with him. I had studied ballet when I was a kid. People don't think of Bob as using ballet as a basis, but he did. There's a wonderful Hirschfeld that appeared when the show opened—all the aspects of Essie Whimple. It's a dream of Essie's where she's a star performer. In the center, they've disguised her so the killer won't find her, and she comes out with a different hair color. Red—what a surprise! Now, I can assure you this was all ballet, but you can see from the way the hands are used that it's not typical ballet. You had to have the training, however, to do it. The pose with the cane and the hat was a cancan and a cakewalk.

Bob choreographed things that were shocking at the time. But I knew enough to do them very straightforwardly, very truthfully. I knew the audience would be a bit shocked. There'd be a moment of shock, then they'd laugh and go "Ohhh." An example: The play took place in London, and Richard Kiley was a real "American"—he smoked a cigar. Now Essie was just floored by this man. When he left, he said goodbye, turned, and let out this huge—and I mean, huge—puff of smoke. And he'd blow it down so it would simply be a cocoon of *his* smoke. Essie would run over, jump inside the smoke, and be enveloped by this man. The audience would scream with delight because they knew how I felt.

Another example I remember. Early in the show, I was still the ugly duckling with my Jane Eyre wig and just goofily in love with Richard Kiley. (I did a lot of jumping around and acting wacky, but I assure you it was choreographed down to where you place your fingers.) Richard, Leonard Stone, and I had just done the song "(Do Something Foolish) Just for Once." They exit, but he had left his glove. (Now, describing this is not the same as seeing it.) I would pick up his glove, put it on my hand, and then put my hand on my breast. Then I'd sing "I Feel Merely Marvelous," and do the dance. For a moment the audience would gasp with pleasure and surprise. Their pleasure made your commitment to it be one hundred percent.

That's another thing I learned. Though no one I studied with taught "being committed" as such, they were so devoted to what they were doing that they would never accept "sort of" doing something. Jack Cole always said that when you go on stage, it should be like the bullfighter in the ring—you either do it right or you get killed. That always made an impression on me. And Bob Fosse was the same: He never expressed it that way, but he was so possessed by what he was doing and by what people were doing of his work that it had to be exact down to the last detail.

"I Shouldn't Sound like Beverly Sills"

I said earlier that I've never been able to really sing, that I could "fake" singing. During those years, and for many afterwards, I studied singing with Keith Davis. I'd go to him once a week. So did Chita. Many other people I knew did, too—pop singers, jazz singers, opera singers. He could give you images about singing. But the most imporant thing he taught me was: Sing on the speaking level, which really pushed a button for me. It meant you're not thinking about notes and going up and down the scale—of course, you have to go up and down, that's what singing is—but think of yourself as speaking it. It makes it more natural. I have what is usually called a "character" voice, and it works for musical theatre because a show is about character, and the voice needs to be real. If I'm playing Essie, I shouldn't sound like Beverly Sills.

Charity Hope Valentine: Sweet Charity

There was great interest in making a musical of Fellini's film *Nights of Cabiria* that starred Guiletta Masina. They showed it to me, and I didn't care for it very much. Here's this poor creature who gets pushed aside and knocked down, and she's so pathetic. The only scene that was truly touching was the one where she picks up a chicken and hugs it. She's so desperate to love something that she rocks this chicken back and forth.

Bob did an adaptation, and I thought it was terrific. Because he knew he couldn't write, direct, and choreograph, Neil Simon joined us and wrote the elevator scene where Oscar (who's claustrophobic) becomes a basket case. He also came up with the idea for "If My Friends Could See Me Now" because all the collaborators felt the first act needed something pleasurable and uplifting for Charity. Another hat and a cane, too.

Along with the words in the script and the songs, I did some research to discover who Charity was. Because she was a dance-hall hostess, I went to dance halls. All those women seemed trapped back in the '30s. They dressed like the '30s. One thought she was Veronica Lake with that hairdo. Another thought she was Lana Turner. And there was one who thought she was Joan Crawford with those plastic shoes. One girl was knitting. I went over to talk to her. "I do this," she explained, "to make enough money to pay for the baby. I'm not due for five months. My husband is in Korea." Because she didn't know how to do anything else, she became a dance-hall hostess. If these women made dates after work as prostitutes, I never found out.

All of that just built the character for me, plus the image of Guiletta hugging that chicken. She just wanted something so badly to love. I know the sign for the show read, "The story of a girl who wanted to be loved." But really, it's the story of a girl who wanted to love someone.

In the original Broadway production—and it's on the album—is the great Act I song, "Charity's Soliloquy." It's about her relation with Charlie. Later it was dropped—on the national tour, the movie, and every other production—because they felt it kept Charlie alive too long. Thank God I had it. She sings:

I left the tip, picked up the tab
For the jockey shorts and the taxi cab . . .
But what do you do when he knocks on your door

'Cause they locked him out of his furnished room?
So he moves in, with his jockey shorts, a paper bag and nothing
else.

She can't resist him, though she knows she should. The song is all about who Charity is and how she feels about herself and men. Dorothy Fields and Cy Coleman wrote the lyrics and the music. Their understanding of the character helped me.

The "Charity" Dress

I started working in the "Charity" dress early on in rehearsal. I had a Norman Norel evening gown, and there was a slip to it. I didn't really need the slip, so I cut it off. I wanted a handbag because there was no time to change between scenes. I tied a rope on it. In that photo, that's the petticoat and my own handbag with a rope. They left it in the show that way, and in the movie, too. Irene Sharaff designed a costume that was very similar. But it was covered with crocheted black balls. They kept falling off and just getting in the way. You could never get a clean line, and you really couldn't sit down in it. And I thought she should be in a uniform, very much like Edith Piaf.

I stole that Charity posture that was used in all the advertising from the perfume salesladies at Bloomingdale's. If you have to stand in heels, your feet start to burn, so you take turns shifting the weight from one foot to another. See, that's what I learned from Olivier. You start with a little bit of a dress, you discover you need a handbag, you discover you have to get off your feet, because, my God, your feet are killing you most of the time. All those details just pile up. Now add them to the lyrics, and it's quite a combination.

See, I just paid close attention to people. I'm sure every actor does. I had seen so many girls, really young, who used foul language. They're not even aware that it's foul because that's all they know. I thought that was perfect for Charity. She doesn't know she's saying these things. She says to the Italian movie star, "If someone says that to me, I'd say, 'Up yours.'" I did the line just like you'd say, "Oh, eat a banana," or "Take a flying leap to the moon." But I happened to say, "Up yours." People have often said that on stage I can say vulgar things, and they don't seem so vulgar, again a kind of innocence.

Integrating Songs and Character

Long before we went into rehearsal, I'd start to learn the lyrics and the music for every song in the show. Sometimes I had a pianist. Sometimes Cy would make a piano dub—just the music. As I learned the dances, I'd realize, "Uh oh, I've got to breathe, I can't sing a phrase that long." And we'd work on it. The important thing in singing and dancing at the same time is to figure out *when* to breathe. It's crucial. There was one place in "If My Friends Could See Me Now" where I was breathing, and Dorothy Fields did not want me to. I was taking a breath before the word *pow* in the line:

Tonight I landed, pow!, right in a pot of jam.

Dorothy wanted me to breathe after *pow*. I just couldn't sing that far without breathing. So I thought, "Okay, I'll breathe when I land, and she won't notice." So I sang,

Tonight I landed,

and as I was landing I took a big, big breath, and my dress exploded. I had no idea that I could breathe that deeply. I mean, the whole dress just popped open. So after that, I didn't breathe quite so vigorously. That's one of the numbers when I'm dancing and singing through the whole thing. It was fun—a character dance—they're the best kind. It was sort of manic, not unlike the "'Erbie Fitch" number in *Redhead*.

The high point for me on *Sweet Charity* was going home at night. I was exhausted from that show. I never knew it when I was on stage, but at the end of the evening, I was just dead. It was the most exhausting show I did because I was much older. I was forty. The most difficult—in terms of acting, singing, and dancing—was *Redhead*. But I was thirty-five when it opened, and there's a big difference between what your body can do at thirty-five and what it can do at forty.

Roxie Hart: Chicago

I spent about thirty years trying to get the rights to *Chicago*. It was originally a play by Maurine Dallas Watkins from the twenties and had been made into a terrible Ginger Rogers movie, with a happy ending. But the basic story was so good. I did a lot of research about the original murders and felt it was fascinating. The decadence in Chicago at that time was appalling. Mama Morton was running a house of prostitution in her jail. All the district leaders would show up to "help these women who had committed these murders," and there were curtains in the cells so they could have sex privately.

I finally called Maurine Watkins—a truly strange women, she was living in a nunnery—and told her I wanted to do it. She said, "To talk about a piece of fluff at this time in our country's history." And I said, "But it's not a piece of fluff. It's about decadence. It's a huge comment on the press itself." And she said, "You're the only person who's ever said that," and she gave us the rights. And, you know what? Right after that, Watergate happened.

Creating that show was so exciting. Bob came up with the idea of a

Greek chorus, which would comment on the action of the scenes. The chorus became what I called the "creepy-crawlies"—all these creepy people watching and commenting from above, "Give 'em the old razzle dazzle," on what we did below. Each actor/singer/dancer wore a basic costume designed by Pat Zipprodt; it was tights, one leg silver, one leg black—very commedia. When we got into rehearsal, Bob had trunks of costumes and props. Using Pat's basic "uniform," the chorus could create their own look for the show—they made up their own characters. And they were creepy.

I particularly enjoyed doing "Roxie" because it was the first time I'd ever known a number quite like that. I got to talk to the audience again. During the vamp to the song, I'd lean over and give someone in the audience the newspaper I'd been reading in the scene. I'd say: "I always wanted my name in the papers." If they wouldn't take it, I'd keep talking, "It's really good. You gotta read it. You gotta know." And I'd say to the audience:

I'm gonna tell you the truth,
Not that the truth really matters.
The thing is, see,
I'm older than I ever intended to be . . .
All my life I wanted to be a dancer in vaudeville . . .
But they always turned me down.
It was always, no.

And it went on like that, and became the song. That was a wonderful number to perform.

Along with "Roxie," I loved the numbers with Chita Rivera. She's fantastic. We'd tried to get a show together since *Can-Can*, which is when we first met. We were friends right off the bat, so when this came around, she played Velma Kelly. Chita has such energy, and also she knows if you're still working on the role. She can see little differences, and she goes right with it. You can see that twinkle in her eye, "Oh, good," she's thinking, "Gwen's working on something new." I mean, she can critique you and work at the same time. Of course, you get such energy from her when she dances with you.

Recreating Choreography
I'm not a choreographer, nor have I ever wanted to be. But I've enjoyed recreating Bob's choreography. Jack Cole and Bob Fosse are my whole dancing past. With Jack, it was my youth. With Bob, I was in my prime. I was old when I did *Chicago*. I was fifty when it opened, so when I left it in 1978, I was fifty-two. To see someone young do that dancing bril-

liantly is thrilling. Allowing an Annie Reinking to bring her own point of view to that dancing is a pleasure. I know when it's being done right. To see that enthusiasm is thrilling. Though it's something I can no longer do physically, emotionally and mentally I still think I'm equipped. So I give it over to them, and it's like doing it myself. I get a vicarious thrill.

It sounds so macabre, but I've said it before: Dancers do die twice; first, when their bodies start to go, and then—. If you're prepared for a life after dancing, it's not so macabre. I wasn't afraid to play somebody's mother—Mia Farrow's in *Alice*, Richard Gere's in *Cotton Club*, and Magnum, P.I.'s. Now in playing Aunt Ruth in the film of *Marvin's Room*, I'm really old—and crippled. Basically, I approched playing Ruth as I would a role on the stage. I learned from Bob about economy, whether it's movement or acting. Even though I couldn't stand the way George Abbott directed—"Just say the words and get off"—he had a point. Do your research and preparation, know who the character is, and then you become the character.

Working on *Marvin's Room* was a joy. Meryl Streep, Diane Keaton, Hume Cronyn—they're all brilliant in it. They are so smart that I felt dumb. So I used my feeling like a dummy. If you've been crippled from the time you've been a child, as Ruth has been, and you've never really had a youth—when you finally get out of pain, well, you start living, you start playing games. You start being a teenager, which does make her seem slightly cuckoo or, really, it's more that she has her innocence for the first time. Ruth would enjoy things in a way she never had before, and express it like a child. She had earned her innocence.

BROADWAY
Chicago (Tony nomination, Best Actress in a Musical); *Children! Children!*, *Sweet Charity* (Tony nomination, Best Actress in a Musical, and Drama Critics Award, Best Actress in a Musical); *Redhead* (Tony Award, Best Actress in a Musical), *New Girl in Town* (Tony Award, Best Actress in a Musical); *Damn Yankees* (Tony Award, Best Actress in a Musical); *Can-Can* (Tony Award, Best Featured Actress in a Musical, and Donaldson Award, Best Female Dancer); *Alive and Kicking*, directed and choreographed by Jack Cole.

NATIONAL TOURS
Chicago, *Redhead*.

FILM
Marvin's Room (Screen Actors' Guild Nominee, Best Supporting Actress), *Alice*, *Cocoon*, *Cotton Club*, *Damn Yankees*, *Mississippi Gambler*, *Meet Me After the Show*, *David and Bathsheba*, *On the Riviera*.

<u>TELEVISION</u>

Episodic: *Magnum, P.I.* (Emmy nomination, Outstanding Guest Performance in a Drama Series), *M*A*S*H*, *Fame*, *All Is Forgiven*, *Trapper John, M.D.*, *The Equalizer*, *Webster*. Film: *Legs*.

<u>SPECIAL AWARDS</u>

Grammy Award, *Redhead*, Outstanding Broadway Cast Recording, 1960; Silver Bowl for Outstanding Dance, 1961 (*Dance* Magazine); Governor's Arts Award, 1989; Honored for Career Achievement, New Dramatists Spring Luncheon, 1993.

"The dress is very staid and proper; it's got the little round collar for Eve White. . . . as I became Eve Black, I unbuttoned the top, took the hat off to let my hair loose, leaned back in the chair, and the way the dress changed helped me to become her."

in *The Three Faces of Eve* with
Lee J. Cobb

PHOTOFEST

Joanne Woodward
An Instinctive Rapport

I met Joanne Woodward for the first time in the summer of 1987 when I was stage-managing a production of Odets' *Golden Boy* that she was directing at the Williamstown Theatre Festival. I felt I was meeting an old friend because I had fallen in love with her thirty years before when I saw her first great film success, *The Three Faces of Eve*. I was about ten years old, and my mother had had a "talk" with me before we saw the film. She wanted to make sure that its subject matter—the emerging of multiple personalities in a woman who was schizophrenic—didn't trouble me unduly. Far from being troubled, I was mesmerized by Joanne Woodward's performance and could talk of nothing else for weeks afterward. Consequently, I never missed one of her films.

Joanne is, of course, internationally known as a film actress, having received, over her forty-five-year career, four Academy Award nominations (she won for *The Three Faces of Eve*), three citations as best actress by the New York Film Critics Circle (*Rachel, Rachel; Summer Wishes, Winter Dreams;* and *Mr. and Mrs. Bridge*), five Emmy nominations with two wins (*See How She Runs* and *Do You Remember Love*), among many other accolades.

To talk about specific film performances of hers is to mention a gallery of fascinating, complex, often unusual but always representative, women she has created. How could one ever forget her flaky self-indulgent Carol Cutrere, opposite Marlon Brando in *The Fugitive Kind*, an adaptation of Tennessee Williams' *Orpheus Descending*, in which she deep-fried her natural Georgia accent (relocating it to Mississippi), covered her face with ghoulish amounts of white powder and black eyeliner, and created a laugh that sounded like firecrackers with a case of bronchitis.

Also unforgettable: Lila Green in *The Stripper*, with her deliciously jiggling walk, a combination of voluptuous swagger and childlike innocence; her wrenching performance as Rita, the unhappy middle-aged New York matron, who, clutching her purse, undergoes a nervous breakdown all alone in the London tubes, in *Summer Wishes, Winter Dreams*; the tortured Beatrice Hunsdorf, a monster mother humanized by Joanne's enormous empathy for her pain, in *The Effect of Gamma Rays on Man-in-the-Moon Marigolds*; her wonderfully direct Elizabeth Huckaby in *Crisis at Central High*, in which she created a truly believable intimacy with Henderson Forsythe who played her husband—there was no doubt they had been married for many years. I could mention here almost every performance she has given because each of them—at the very least—has moments of instinctive greatness (see what she does with a forty-five-second telephone call in her memorable turn as Tom Hanks' mother in *Philadelphia*); and many of them are completely brilliant (her beautifully modulated performance as India Bridge in *Mr. and Mrs. Bridge*). To say too much more here, though, would detract from what Joanne Woodward says about the performances herself.

Because her film career has kept her so busy, she is less well known as a theatre actress, and that's a great loss to the public because she is superb on stage. "I don't know any other actor whose instincts are as pure as Joanne's," Paul Newman, her husband and frequent collaborator, said to me in 1988. I think as an actress she is incapable of lying. Perhaps she can be misdirected, or misguided, but the purity of her basic instincts is so strong, she transcends whatever interferences are around and manages to take you with her emotionally wherever she wants to go. I remember a vivid instance.

It was the last day of the New York rehearsals for a revival of Tennessee Williams' *Sweet Bird of Youth* that was to be performed at Toronto's Royal Alexandra Theatre. Joanne was playing Alexandra Del Lago (the Princess Kosmonopolis) opposite the Chance Wayne of Terry Kinney. Watching her in the three-week rehearsal period had felt like a huge gift. This great performer for whom I'd had so much cultural affection for over thirty years has a wonderful theatricality and spiritedness, a quality that's always set her apart without undermining her natural instinctive gifts. Watching her day-by-day growth into the Princess—picking a detail here and dropping one there, adding a bit of business with a cigarette lighter as she smoked hash smuggled into the room by Chance, examining her still-beautiful but time-worn face in the mirror and looking away with a mingling of terror and disgust—was a heavenly experience for anyone who loves actors and the acting process.

Towards the end of Act I, which is essentially a ferocious pas-de-deux between the Princess and Chance, Joanne unleashed a fury that showed the torment, pain, and self-disgust of this woman who is a true iron butterfly: emotionally fragile but so innately strong that, at the end of the play, she's the only character who manages to survive, head essentially unbowed. As Joanne threw herself across the room at Chance, as if to attack him with her entire being, the lighting designer, Curt Osterman, who was sitting next to me, grabbed my arm, and without realizing he was speaking at all, said, "My God, that's an actress!"

I don't remember now if that particular moment stayed in the production, but it was indicative of the emotional fullness with which Joanne Woodward commits herself to a role.

Choosing a Role

I have no specifics when it comes to why I want to do a role. It's a sensation. Well, that's not entirely true. Sometimes you read a script and there are very specific reasons. Sometimes it's not the role, it's the piece itself. And I think to myself, "This has something to say that I think should be said, and I want to say it." Which was the case, for instance, recently with the film *Breathing Lessons*. I love Anne Tyler's work. I loved that character, Maggie Moran, and I loved the whole ambience of that piece. So, in that instance, it wasn't really the character. That's a character I've played variations on many times. I just liked the sweetness of it, its humanity. And sometimes I have no idea why I want to play something. It speaks to my condition, as they used to say.

Occasionally, my choice of roles is something of an aberration, I'm sure. I really don't think I wanted to play the Princess in *Sweet Bird of Youth*. That was one of those times when I thought, "Nobody would ever cast me in this part," so I really wanted to do it to show them I could. It was like, why do you want to climb a mountain? Because it's there.

In this business, whatever you make your initial impact as stays with you for a very long time. And since I started out doing things like *The*

Three Faces of Eve and the pyschiatrist in *Sybil*, I think people think of me as playing (a) slightly eccentric but usually fragile and delicate creatures, and (b) wonderful, warm, sincere, caring people. The Princess is neither of those. She may be underneath. So for me playing the Princess was a curiosity.

Sometimes a particular playwright is a factor in my choosing a role. I would be happy to do anything of Tennessee's, and if Horton Foote handed me a script tomorrow, I'm sure I'd want to do it because I love his plays. My first roles in television forty years ago were Horton's work. And also being southern, I relate to him. Horton and I have the same feelings about things. It would not occur to me, however, to do some playwrights, though I admire them. For instance, though I did one many years ago, I cannot imagine doing an Arthur Miller play. He writes characters that I wouldn't feel comfortable playing, or wouldn't feel I could bring anything to.

Pre-rehearsal Work

Once I've chosen a role, the work I do before rehearsals begin is probably the most important part. I do what Sandy Meisner used to recommend when I studied with him at the Neighborhood Playhouse. (It made more sense to me than anything I ever heard from Lee Strasberg. Lee's techniques were more intellectual, too specific for me.) Sandy used to say you should just daydream about the part. Don't sit down to start memorizing. Don't start writing questions and asking yourself things—unless that works for you. If it doesn't, he said that daydreaming is a perfectly good tool, particularly if you start to daydream in the sense of the character.

Abby Brewster in *Arsenic and Old Lace*, which I did recently at the Long Wharf, was an interesting character to daydream about. I began to think about who she was, and it became like dreaming about why this little lady had never married, what she felt about her sister, and about her basic innocence; and then of course about her very clear insanity. Where did all this come from? Joyce Ebert (who played Martha) and I talked about the two sisters. Joyce used to laugh at me because I had this theory: At first I thought they should be twins and that we should dress alike. We could have carried that off. Actually we did end up dressing somewhat alike.

Another part of my preparation is working out a history of the character. Otherwise, what do you have to think about when you're on stage? Also, as human beings we all have a history. I mean, when you ask me a question, I don't just answer your question. I answer it in relation to who I am, what I am, and really my whole life. It's very helpful if you can do that with a character, and I find it very difficult with some. For instance, it was very difficult with the Princess. I tried to make a history, but it was hard for me to dissociate myself from having seen Paul and Gerry Page play it so many times in 1959. Consequently, I never felt comfortable, which is probably why a lot of it didn't work for me. I never felt I had examined the character so well that I was at home every moment. There were some places where I'd be fine, and then I'd come to other places where the play doesn't work as well, that second act which is messy. Some people feel that *Sweet Bird of Youth* would be much better if the second act didn't exist, and they're probably right. It's really those two people in that dynamic. In the second act, you lose them.

An Image of the Character

An image of the character is very important to me. All the specific details you've amassed while you were daydreaming contribute to this image. That was another reason why many of the things that Lee taught at the Actors Studio (at least as I understood them) didn't work for me—too strict. Sandy was much looser. His whole conception was that acting was play. Play, play, have a wonderful time, and I'd play around with all those details to get an image of the character. For instance, the glasses for the Princess came because I always lose my own glasses so I need to know specifically where they are. The Princess was just blind as a bat, so she absolutely has to have her glasses no matter how drunk she is. She's got to have them so close by that they're attached.

The image I had of the Princess was of a movie star from the '40s, and it was Rita Hayworth. I probably picked her—and I'm not sure I did this consciously—because (a) I had the red wig and I knew what I wanted it to look like. I thought, "God, yes, it's Rita Hayworth in *Cover Girl* with all that flowing hair." And (b) As she got older and more fragile, Rita was so unsure of herself. She ended up with Alzheimer's, though she worked up until she couldn't remember lines. It was very sad. People didn't know what was wrong with her; they thought she was drunk. I always thought of the Princess as having the fragility of someone beautiful and so unsure of herself who, inside, has the heart of a little lamb, beating furiously. The Princess is terrified of life, of getting old, of everything really, and in her heart is about ten-and-a-half years old.

I was never satisfied with that performance. That second act drove me crazy. I never knew what to do with her there, and I don't think Nikos (Psacharopoulos, who directed it) knew either. He was not, at least for me, helpful with the Princess. I think he knew it and felt bad because he certainly would have wanted to be helpful.

As I investigate a character, I don't really do a lot of "formal" research (though finding the character's history is a form of it). Maybe part of the reason is I've never done anything that really necessitated much research. I know a lot of people do. Paul loves to—always did—and he does a lot of it. That's not what I hook into. I'd be more likely to try to find the right hat. For instance, the hats I wore in *Mr. and Mrs. Bridge* showed so much about character, which is what costumes should always do. I picked those hats out because I was so attuned to India Bridge. She was so much like the women I knew in my childhood, though she was not southern. All those wonderful ladies in the hats and gloves. I had a great hat in the first scene in Paris—that's where we shot first. When we're walking along in Paris, the white hat that hangs over the side of her head—it shows her and hides her at once. Then there's the one in the car at the end of the film—it was maroon; it sits on her head just so, and has that funny little feather that wiggled. She's trapped in the Lincoln, looking out the window with snow falling all around. She's so uncertain. And the hat sits firmly on her head, and the feather moved slightly. Tenuous and tenacious like India herself. See what I mean about hats?

Rehearsal

I don't do a lot of work on the text beforehand, other than, as I said, daydream about it. I don't even look at the script a lot, mainly because I don't want to be in a position of learning things too early. I don't want to look at lines because that makes them "lines." So I read the script once or twice. Sometimes I don't read it the night before. My tendency in a first readthrough (which a lot of people would disagree with) is to perform. I love it. It's fun. When you sit around a table, you can go far, maybe too far, because it doesn't matter. Later, I may find that what I did was wrong, and I may go to something entirely different, but it's interesting to just go for it. And sometimes it works. Sometimes you find things in the first reading that will always be there for you. Many details will change but some things you find right away and they stay.

After the readthrough, I don't *seem* to do much work for the first few days. You know, Joey Tillinger, who directed *Arsenic and Old Lace*, had never worked with me before, and my not seeming to do anything must have been a shock. Once I get up and start moving around, I have to have at least a week of just stumbling, not trying to pull it together. I am a little like Frankenstein. You know, the monster is trying to get up and walk, and he has a terrible time. That's me the first week or so. I do try to relate to other people and have some sense of where I am, who I am. Sometimes things don't make any sense to me until the second week.

As I work, the intentions of the character are mostly unconscious. Usually, if what I've been daydreaming about in the character—who the character is—feels fairly comfortable in rehearsal, then the intentions happen of themselves, especially if it's a good play.

If the play is not as good, it's another story. For instance, in that second act of *Sweet Bird*, I could never find the right intentions. I could always find "intellectual" intentions, but those are lousy because you have to arbitrarily get yourself into it. Sometimes later on in the rehearsal process I find I'm wrong, and the director may say, "How about this?" or "How about that?" and I'll think, "Oh, my God, of course! I never thought about that." But by and large, the intentions in the scene are as simple as "Why do you walk in the door?"

For instance, the first scene of *Arsenic and Old Lace* starts in the middle of a conversation and, of course, it sets up what the entire play is about. It took me several weeks into the run of the play to get it. I kept forgetting lines, which I rarely do. I thought, "There's something wrong. What am I doing wrong here?" And then I finally found an overall intention for the first scene. After I found it, it was such a relief because then I knew what she was doing and why. Of course, the audience response, or lack of it, helps you get it, too. That's why previews are so important. The audience tells you a lot.

I love rehearsals because you can play. In a good rehearsal situation, ideally, the other actors would be on the same wavelength I'm on. It doesn't always happen. In fact, rarely does it happen, since I have such weird wavelengths. At least if the actors are looking at you. It drives me crazy if they're not. That's why it was difficult working with Olivier on that British television version of *Come Back Little Sheba*. And I adored him. He was brilliant as Doc, Lola's alcoholic husband, and partly I think because that situation of a drinker is something he knew well. At the time, he was very fragile. But there was no way that we could communicate, and so it was a tough experience for me. Perhaps he chose that—not communicating. But I sure never knew it. He was fairly much to himself by that time.

Of course, a good rehearsal situation depends on who you've got. Rehearsing *Mr. and Mrs. Bridge*, for instance, was ideal because James Ivory likes, as nearly as I can gather, to hire actors whom he knows and whom he knows can do their job. He doesn't deal with rehearsing, and that can be a very relaxing thing: you find it for yourselves. Though there were moments on that film when I felt a little lost, Jim was wonderful about allowing us the rehearsal time to find it all. And the other actors we had, especially in the family—Bob Leonard, Kyra Sedgwick, Margaret Welsh, and that beautiful actress who played the cook, Saundra McClain—were wonderful. We developed a real relationship as a family.

I love the scene where Blythe Danner is telling India how worried she is about her mind, and I just can't quite get it. Blythe and I never, ever talked about what the scene was about. It's marvelous to have somebody like that with whom to work. I don't like to talk about it when I'm acting because it makes it unreal. I never like talking about a film while I'm doing it, either.

In terms of directors, everybody has been useful in a different way. I don't think I've ever worked with a stage director who's not been useful at all. I think immediately of Larry Sacharow, who is so dreamy. We were doing *The Seagull*. And initially I thought, "Jesus, isn't he going to be helpful here at all? Isn't he going to say something?" That play is hard. You really have to do the work there; you can't just wander in off the street and try to make it work. You have to have your life going. What Larry did was just allow us to do it. And I think that very often is the best possible thing. The easiest people to work with are the ones who are the simplest. Joey Tillinger is like that. Joey doesn't do a lot. He more or less lets you find it, and then gives little hints here and there. And, you know, if you find it yourself, it stays with you.

I don't consciously use things from my own life anymore. There was a time, you know, when I was fresh out of drama school—and one was using sense memory and all that—I think I did. If I do now it's because it simply happens that way. I'm older now and have a whole life experience, and so almost anything I'm doing relates in some way to something. Sandy used to say, "It takes twenty years to be an actor. It's like being a violinist. You have to get to a point where you don't think about where you put your fingers." It's the same way with acting. My life is just a tool that's there now.

If I had to categorize myself, I'd have to say that I'm basically instinctive. Intellectual I am not, and that's one of the reasons that technique is hard to talk about it and why I was hesitant when you asked me for the first book. I felt I had no technique. Sandy used to say, "The method is whatever works for you." Paul and I work in an entirely different way. We work very well together, but we're certainly different in our approach.

It occured to me in reading your book that Bobby Leonard is a much more concise actor in terms of his technique than I am. But I've rarely worked with an actor with whom I had a greater rapport, and I'm talking about an instinctive rapport. There were scenes we did together in *Mr. and Mrs. Bridge*, and we didn't talk about anything at all. He found his character and I found mine, and we both knew what the relationship was. It's very much in the Boy Scout scene where he struggles about whether to kiss India, and then he's embarrassed as he almost stoops to kiss me. We didn't talk about that. It just happened. That's instinctive technique, I suppose—maybe the most important kind.

Costumes and Character: "The Clothes Make a Big Difference"

Whatever costumes I wear affect to a great degree what happens to the character. I have found myself sometimes simply destroyed by the wrong costume. The first time I played Amanda in *The Glass Menagerie*, for instance. I was in my early forties—perhaps an odd age to play it but not wrong—and I had a strong sense of what I wanted to do with it. I felt, if I'm Amanda, there's no reason why I can't look like I look, except in period. I had gotten a blond wig that looked a little like Laurette Taylor's. And I also wanted to play it in the '30s wardrobe, wearing clothes that Amanda would have worn ten to fifteen years before because she couldn't afford new ones.

This was done in Greenville, South Carolina. Because of complicated schedules, I had learned the part alone. I had one week's rehearsal with the cast who had already been in rehearsal for a number of weeks with someone else playing Amanda. Dear Bob McLane (who was my professor from years ago and a wonderful mentor) had picked out a horrible Victorian wig and Victorian wardrobe. I begged him not to do it, but he just couldn't understand why I didn't think this was a wonderful thing to do. It must have been one of the worst Amandas ever. I felt I was encased in armor. It was awful. So, my point is that the clothes make a big difference.

When I'm doing a play, the designer is usually somebody I know or somebody I've worked with before, so we'll have a sense of what it's about. David Murin, who designed the clothes for *Arsenic and Old Lace*, had exactly the right thing in mind. The one thing I said was that I thought Joyce and I should dress rather alike—that they are two halves of the same person—and he got that right away. I said that I thought Abby is stuck in a time warp. She's really about sixteen. I had worked out that she had one suitor, and the suitor had been killed in World War I. This may have been the thing that pushed her over the edge, but it also stopped her at that point in time. I wore a ring that my suitor had given me. I wanted her clothes to reflect all that. Martha's clothes were a little more dignified—she was more the mother figure—and Abby's were more fanciful and girlish.

In the instance of *Sweet Bird of Youth*, the blue-sequined dress that Jess Goldstein designed was stunning. He and I talked about having something that was like what Rita Hayworth would have worn. You know, one of those Hollywood dresses that had what I call a "life of

Sweet Bird of Youth.
Princess Kosmonopolis.
Act II, sc. 2.
Joanne Woodward.

"The blue-sequined dress that Jess Goldstein designed was stunning. He and I talked about having something that was like what Rita Hayworth would have worn . . . one of those Hollywood dresses that had what I call 'a life of their own.' It worked because it's a movie-star dress."
Costume Design
by Jess Goldstein.

Act II, Scene 2, The Princess, Sweet Bird
of Youth

their own." It worked because it's a movie-star dress. It was perfect, a meeting of the minds of Jess and me. That dress and her red hair clarified for me who that woman was.

A "Prop" Actress

I've been accused of being a "prop" actress, and it's true—to an extent. I love objects that have to do with the character, like the broken glasses for the Princess. In *Arsenic and Old Lace*, I had glasses that were on a chain. You couldn't tell at first what they were because Abby was vain and didn't want anyone to know she needed them. Of course, it became a wonderful prop. The first time I used them was when the Frankenstein character comes in. Props like that are very necessary.

When I was doing the film *Breathing Lessons*, I had a complicated knitting pattern that I did while we were driving. I don't know if it was ever seen, but it helped me get closer to who Maggie was. She also had the little curls on the side of her head, and I kept taking off my clips and putting them back on. I also had a purse that had packets of crackers she had taken from various restaurants—my mother used to do that. Props, too, will tell you what the life is around the character. India Bridge didn't have props, but then she didn't have much of a life.

Acting in Film

Acting in front of a camera is purgatory. To do it, I have to put myself in a kind of trance. I cannot pal around with people on the set. I generally stay in my trailer, I don't talk to people, and I hate being forced into situations where I have to. Or if I do it, I have to do it in character. In *Breathing Lessons*, I found it was all right to be chatty with people because Maggie was so friendly. It was, in its way, a means of being in character. I suppose that acting in films has to do with an intense concentration. Ninety percent is concentration, and the only way for me to do it is to stay by myself.

Of course, you shoot out-of-sequence—mostly—and that doesn't help much. When we were doing *Breathing Lessons*, the first scene we shot (and it was after only two days of rehearsal around a table with Jim Garner and Katie Erbe who played my husband and daughter) was in the cafe with Eileen Heckart and me. We rehearsed it briefly and then we shot it. Fortunately, Heckie and I had worked together since the Broadway production of *Picnic* in the '50s. But it was hard—to begin on the first day of shooting with a scene in the middle of the script. If I didn't go up, she did. We were a mess for a while.

The Three Faces of Eve

I got the role in *The Three Faces of Eve*, really, by the process of elimination. It was produced by 20th Century Fox, and everything was on schedule in those days. They had offered it to Judy Garland and June Allyson, and I think, Carroll Baker. Everybody turned it down. I was under contract to 20th, and I didn't have a chance to turn it down. I was coming out to California to do *The Wayward Bus*. My agent sent over a script, and I read it on the Broadway Limited from New York to Chicago. I got off the train in Chicago, called my agent, and said, "You're crazy. I don't have any idea what this is about. I don't want to do this picture. I want to do *The Wayward Bus* with my friend Joan Collins." And they said, "Sorry, this is the one you're doing. Start learning the lines. You begin shooting in a week."

I remember Nunnally Johnson, who wrote and directed it, asking me if I would prefer to shoot in sequence or shoot the different characters in sequence—you know, all of Eve White, then all of Eve Black. And I said, "No, I'd like to shoot in sequence." I don't know why because at that point I had no ideas of how to do the role at all. It all happened so quickly, and believe me, I had no idea what I was doing. It was truly instinct. When I got there, Nunnally (whom I'd never met before) said, "Honey, can you do a southern accent?" And I said, "Yes," and he said, "Thank God."

This was before there was any real rehearsal for films. So Lee Cobb, who was playing Dr. Luther, and I went to see the film of the real Eve, which had been made for the American Psychiatric Association. And all I could think, as I watched her go from one personality to another, was, "How am I going to do that?" During my first costume fitting (that's how rushed it was—we discussed character at a fitting), Nunnally and I talked about how to do the transformations from Eve White to Eve Black. I told him that I felt the way the real woman changed was very rapid, and if I did it that way, it was going to seem funny. So we felt I should do something to slow down the change a little, especially at the beginning. As the film goes on, the changes get less slow. So that's how the lowering of the head came to be.

My costumes for that film were especially good, and oddly, all but two were pulled from stock. The dress that Eve White wears the first time she goes to see Dr. Luther was designed for me. We knew I had to wear that dress for a long time—it's that whole first sequence in his office. I think it was probably the designer Renie's idea to have something that was so flexible. She got the idea for it from Fortuni dresses—they were very famous, they had the little pleats. And she found that fabric, I think it was some form of crepe. The dress is very staid and proper; it's got the little round collar for Eve White. I remember that as I became Eve Black I unbuttoned the top, took the hat off to let my hair loose, leaned back in the chair, and the way the dress changed helped me to become her. The other dress that was designed was the red one—oh, I always forget it's not in color—it was a red velvet dress, all sequins and open down the back, that Eve Black wears when she goes out on the town. That's the dress I'm talking about in the last scene when I'm so confused I think I may not live, and say to Dr. Luther, "If I die, I want you to have that red dress."

We shot the film in 1956, and I'd been out of the Neighborhood Playhouse since 1952. One of the things I really related to was what Martha Graham taught there. Martha, of course, always felt that everything came from the body, and that the body moves because of emotion. I can't remember whether it was Martha or Louis Horst—he taught a course called Pre-Classic Dance Forms, but it was really teaching us how to move. Martha believed that it all comes from *here* [indicating the diaphragm], and that you begin there with everything.

So I decided that the only way I could possibly make this work was to find three different ways of moving, and if I moved a certain way it would reverse itself into the emotions. Eve White had a certain way of holding herself, and then when she becomes Eve Black the posture becomes quite different. If you sit slumped inward, it gives you a different way of talking, and that affects everything else. Eve White holds her bag in her lap, and it's all about containment and self-protection. Eve Black lounges back and the bag is hanging off her arm. That tells us something completely different.

If I could do it again, I would change Jane, the one the two Eves merge into and become. I never liked her very much. I found her a little priggish. You know, you think, "What a nice girl!" Now I would have tried to think of something to make her a little more real. I think it was probably just what it should have been. I was so unsure, it was very terrifying.

The worst was filming the last long sequence where all three personalities keep emerging and changing back and forth. Actually, we shot most of that in one take. Again, Nunnally asked me if I wanted to do that, and Lee and I decided that it would be a lot easier to sustain the emotional ups and downs to do it in one shot. So we played it all together—it was about seven or eight pages of dialogue. And Nunnally was wonderful about allowing us to rehearse it as much as we needed before we shot it. And so we shot it, and it was devastating. I mean, I was a wreck. At the end of it, the camera operator came over to me and said, "Joanne, I'm sorry, there's a hair in the aperture." I burst into tears, just distraught. And Lee, who was so great, sat me down and said, "Oh, for Christ's sake, Joanne, if you did it once, you can do it again." So we shot the whole thing again, and of course it was better. Anyway, it was what it was, and I don't think I'd want to do it again.

Over the years, several people have complimented me on the subtlety of that final sequence. And it was good probably because Lee and I were working in totally the same way. We really did have an enormously good relationship. Another actor with whom I had the same experience—you know, one of those times you find an actor with whom you just connect—was Austin Pendleton in *Mr. and Mrs. Bridge*. We had such a special relation. Especially the scene where he's selling the subscription to the Doberman magazine. It was one of those magical afternoons when we shot it. We were totally in sync. I'd love to work with him again.

The Long Hot Summer

I've been told that *The Long Hot Summer* has come to have one of those "reputations" because of the dialogue. It was a marvelous script, written by that couple, Irving Ravetch and Harriet Frank, Jr. Paul was playing Ben Quick—it was our first film together, though we'd worked together on Broadway in *Picnic* and done an early live television drama. The dialogue is ripe:

> Ben: You slam the door in a man's face before he even opens it.
> Clara: I got *no* written all over my face.
> Ben: That don't bother me a bit. Lots of women say no when they mean yes.

Later:

> Clara: Wild horses wouldn't drag me off this porch.
> Ben: You got a bigger appetite than that.

Quite spicy for 1958. Several people have said to me over the years that it's a sexy movie. Well, we were just so sexy ourselves that it needed very little to bring it out. We weren't married yet, but on location we were hopping back and forth between each other's bedrooms. You know, though, whatever the dialogue, you have to play the intentions.

The Stripper

What a mess they made of *The Stripper*! It was Frank Shaffner's first film, and it was based on Bill Inge's play *A Loss of Roses*. The script was written by a friend of mine, Meade Roberts. We got to rehearse. It was one of the few times that Dick Beymer was well cast and very good. Claire Trevor as his mother was so good. Oh God, I loved that part— Lila Green. One thing I was aware of as I worked on her was that she was so childlike. We invented a wonderful prop for her: that teddy bear that I held onto. There's a vulnerability and resilience in Lila that I tried to capture in her walk.

Billy Travilla designed my wardrobe, and he had a great sense of character and style. We decided right at the beginning that (a) it was an homage to Marilyn (who was still alive), and (b) a specific homage to

Lana Turner in *The Postman Always Rings Twice*. That film was black and white, and everything she wore was white, her hair was white-blonde, and she had that suntan. So all the costumes were designed with that in mind. I had them make fake bosoms for me because I wanted them to bobble up and down when I walked.

We had a wonderful time rehearsing. The script was charming. Meade had done a good job on it. About halfway through shooting, our producer Jerry Wald died. He was a good friend, so we were devastated. Darryl Zanuck came to see the rough cut. At the end of it, he didn't speak to Frank Shaffner. He just turned to the assistant and said, "Where are the outtakes?" Frank was summarily thrown off the film, and Zanuck, who knew nothing about it, recut it. He said, "She can't sing and dance," so he cut almost all the dancing. Of course she can't, that's the point. They cut the scene where I tried to slit my wrists, so I'm going around in the last scene with a bandage on my wrist and there's no explanation for why. It doesn't make sense.

The film has often been called, I guess the word is, *atrope* on Marilyn Monroe. The final thing that happpened just before they released the film: Marilyn died. So they cut out the references to her. For instance, the opening when I'm walking down the street and someone says, "Who's that? It looks like Marilyn Monroe," and someone else says, "No, that's nobody." They changed it to "Jayne Mansfield," and it just wasn't right. I'm still sorry that one was so badly botched.

Rachel, Rachel

Rachel Cameron—a character to die for. More than anything, it was the right part for me to play, at the right time. Rachel says, "I'm at the exact middle of my life." She was thirty-five. I was thirty-seven. John Foreman, I think, found the book, and we got Stewart Stern to write the screenplay. As long as I live, I'll never forgive the Academy for not giving him the Oscar for writing it.

The filming itself was absolute heaven. Paul was directing. My daughter Nellie was playing me as a little girl. Everybody in it was so good. Estelle Parsons was wonderful. Jimmy Olsen, too. The lovemaking scene, which was discussed a lot when the film came out in 1968, was completely from her point of view, and it made you understand her better. It was the turning point in her life. You know, there was nothing in that movie that wasn't completely necessary to it. Almost everything we shot is in the final film. The three of us—Paul, Stewart, and myself—worked together so long on it. It was a truly magic time. I don't think I've ever had a better experience.

The Effect of Gamma Rays on Man-in-the-Moon Marigolds

Beatrice Hunsdorf in *The Effect of Gamma Rays on Man-in-the-Moon Marigolds*. Oh my, that was one I didn't want to do. And I only did it because Paul wanted to direct me in it. We went to see the play downtown, and I thought, "God, what a miserable, hateful woman." Paul had a very difficult mother, and the only thing I can figure is somehow he related to that story. I don't know what he was telling me about myself. But he bought it for me and was determined I was going to do it. I fought it every step of the way. We almost got a divorce over that one, I swear to God.

It was very hard to do every day. She's so unpleasant, and I'm intuitive. So it made me depressed all the time. I was just miserable. I hated being so mean, and I hated being so mean to my own child, Nell, who was playing my daughter. When I came staggering down the aisle, drunk, saying, "My heart is so full," there's a closeup of Nell that's heartbreaking. I thought, "What have I done? She'll never forgive me." A few days ago I was reminded that I won the acting award that year at the Cannes Film Festival. I hated being at the Festival so badly that I made Paul go by himself and accept it for me. The only nice thing about it was Nell was simply wonderful, and Roberta Wallach, who was playing the older daughter, was, too.

Summer Wishes, Winter Dreams

Stewart Stern also wrote *Summer Wishes, Winter Dreams*. It was about his mother and father and him. Rhoda is a wonderful character. What happens to her—that breakdown of sorts—in the London subway is so affecting. She's really a forerunner of Mrs. Bridge, sort of a sophisticated, New York Mrs. Bridge. I can see why it wasn't more successful. It's pretty bleak. But I loved doing it because it was so inner. That is a woman, like India, who had things happen *to* her. She rarely instigated anything. She was pretty much at the mercy of her mother, her daughter, the son, the husband. It was a challenge to play it because it's almost a totally reactive role.

Do You Remember Love

An early draft of *Do You Remember Love* was sent to me, and though the subject was important—a woman and her family undergoing the effects of Alzheimer's—it really wasn't very good. But the director Jeff Bleckner kept saying, "Please do it." And they had Dick Kiley playing the husband, and I love working with Dick. So I said, yes. Anyway, we worked on the script, endlessly, right up to the last minute. We improvised a lot of it. There's a scene in the kitchen. I'm at the point where I'm forgetting many things, and I can't remember something, and my husband gets angry. Finally, we both break down laughing. It was almost completely improvised. And it worked.

The Glass Menagerie

I don't know about *The Glass Menagerie*. Paul and I have talked about that because he had an idea, and I didn't necessarily agree with it. He didn't want to open it up; he just wanted it to be Tennessee's play, pure and simple. His feeling was that it was a memory and that you tend to soften things in the memory.

I felt he tempered my performance. I've only seen it once, and there were a number of things I'm unsure of: I thought, for instance, I looked too romantic. A perfectly valid way to play it, but I preferred the way I had done it on stage at Williamstown and Long Wharf. It was much tougher. I'll never forget Nikos (who directed it on stage) saying to me with his inimitable Greek accent, "You want to play it like dis, like dis," with a lot of intensity and anger. He was afraid that Amanda would get soft and easy.

I've played it four times now, and frankly, a lot of its success depends on who's playing Tom. The easiest to play it with, curiously enough, was John Sayles. He had not been on stage since college and he was terrified. Because he was so impenetrable, I didn't know who he was, or what he was. It was frustrating because I couldn't get to him, and that worked very well for me. John Malkovich, of course,

"She's trapped in the Lincoln, looking out the window with snow falling all around. She's so uncertain. And the hat sits firmly on her head, and the feather moved slightly. Tenuous and tenacious like India herself."
Photo by Mikki Ansin.

Joanne Woodward as India Bridge
in Mr. and Mrs. Bridge.

was very interesting. He was wonderfully irritating. But it didn't allow one the desperation of trying to get through to someone. So I have a feeling that Amanda is very often dependent on who's playing Tom opposite her.

Mr. and Mrs. Bridge

Playing India Bridge in *Mr. and Mrs. Bridge* was a joy. I'd wanted to get that filmed for nearly twenty years, ever since I first read the two Evan Connell novels on which the film is based. India is a woman I understand from my own childhood, and to create her was a pleasure. And Paul was wonderful as Walter. Many people have mentioned the scene in the kitchen early in the film. The intimacy we create. India comes into the kitchen; Walter's at the kitchen table drinking a beer. She tells him she's had her horoscope read. He's not too interested. India says she's going to get a divorce and she leaves the room. Almost immediately she comes back in. He offers her a beer, she declines, and then she sits on his lap and rests her head on his shoulder. A moment both universal and intimate.

Well, familiarity may breed contempt, but it can also breed good working conditions. I know there are actors who are married who don't, or can't, work well together. There's got to be something wrong with the marriage. Look at Jessie and Hume. I think if you have a good marriage, you have the inner rapport that makes the right things happen.

BROADWAY
Candida, *Baby Want a Kiss*, *The Lovers*, *Picnic*.

REGIONAL
Hay Fever, *Arsenic and Old Lace* directed by John Tillinger; *Sweet Bird of Youth* directed by Nikos Psacharopoulos; *The Glass Menagerie* with John Sayles, Long Wharf Theatre, directed by Nikos Psacharopoulos; *Candida*, *The Seagull*, directed by Lawrence Sacharow; among many others.

FILM
Count Three and Pray, *A Kiss Before Dying*, *The Three Faces of Eve* (Academy Award, National Board of Review, and Golden Globe Award, Best Actress); *No Down Payment* (National Board of Review, Best Actress); *The Long Hot Summer*; *Rally 'Round the Flag, Boys*; *The Fugitive Kind*; *The Sound and the Fury*; *From the Terrace*; *Paris Blues*; *A New Kind of Love*; *The Stripper*; *A Big Hand for the Little Lady*; *A Fine Madness*; *Rachel, Rachel* (Academy Award nomination, Best Actress; New York Film Critics Award, Best Actress; Golden Globe Award, Best Actress); *Winning, WUSA*; *They Might Be Giants*; *The Effect of Gamma*

Rays on Man-in-the-Moon Marigolds (Best Actress, Cannes Film Festival); *Summer Wishes, Winter Dreams* (Academy Award nomination, Best Actress; New York Film Critics Award, Best Actress); *The Drowning Pool*; *The End, Harry and Son*; *The Glass Menagerie*; *Mr. and Mrs. Bridge* (Academy Award nomination, Best Actress; New York Film Critics Award, Best Actress); *Philadelphia*; *The Age of Innocence* (Narrator).

TELEVISION

Series: Guest appearances on *GE Theater, Alcoa Hour, Studio One, Playhouse 90, Omnibus, Alfred Hitchcock Presents, Philco Playhouse, Goodyear Playhouse, Kraft Theater,* among many other episodic shows. Films: *All the Way Home, Sybil (*Emmy nomination, Best Actress), *Come Back Little Sheba, A Christmas to Remember, See How She Runs* (Emmy Award, Best Actress), *The Streets of L.A., The Shadow Box, Crisis at Central High* (Emmy nomination, Best Actress), *Passions, Do You Remember Love* (Emmy Award, Best Actress), *Foreign Affairs, Blind Spot, Breathing Lessons* (Emmy nomination, Best Actress).

Afterword

The eight women interviewed in the preceding pages are actors of the highest quality and the greatest diversity. Their careers span the last fifty-five years, beginning in the final full term of President Franklin Delano Roosevelt—Gwen Verdon danced professionally for the first time in 1942—and continuing up to the present moment. As of this writing, Donna Murphy and Sarah Jessica Parker are starring in musicals on Broadway—Ms. Murphy in *The King and I* and Ms. Parker as Winnifred the Woebegone in *Once Upon a Mattress*. All eight of them have given millions of people immense pleasure, and they will undoubtedly continue to do so.

What struck me profoundly as I reread these interviews recently was that these actresses are also notable educators. Their careers, as embodied in these interviews, teach us that acting technique is, first, very various, and, second, very personal. Joanne Woodward quotes Sanford Meisner, head of New York's Neighborhood Playhouse, as saying once in a class, "The 'Method' is whatever works for you."

Using their own intelligence and ingenuity, and aided by various approaches they have studied—the method as taught by Lee Strassberg at the Actors Studio in New York; acting technique as taught by the Stella Adler Institute; and that taught by Uta Hagen (and others) at The HB Studios; and the many variations of these approaches taught all over the country—these eight actresses have each found their own way of accomplishing what Dion Boucicault described as the essence of acting: the ability "to be the part; to be it in your arms, your legs; to be what you are acting, to be it all over."

Look, for instance, at what each describes as the reason for choosing to play a role. Cherry Jones must feel a "visceral" connection to the character. Because she sees acting as a "public service," Judith Ivey needs to feel the play is "profound" in "some important aspect." In agreement with her is Mary McDonnell, who feels the play has to "say something about the world itself, or society, or the individual in society, or the politics of the time, or the gender politics of the time." Donna Murphy and Sarah Jessica Parker share the same reason though it's expressed differently: Ms. Murphy bases her decision on the quality of "the material, the character, and the story" and Ms. Parker describes it as "the text, the people, and the part." Mary Alice has a similar feeling but is in touch with a more pragmatic aspect. She asks herself, "Do I want to play this character eight times a week?"

The work done on a role before rehearsals begin is an area of fascinating sameness and difference among the eight women. Cherry Jones and Sarah Jessica Parker, for instance, don't do much conscious pre-rehearsal homework. They read the play, and like Judith Ivey, "begin to think about the character." In addition to reading the play, Joanne Woodward begins to "daydream" as the character—a technique taught her by Sanford Meisner. Donna Murphy does a "huge amount of research" on the background, the historical period, and whatever may arise with which she is unfamiliar. Look at the discussion of her research on Anna in *The King and I*, and the fascinating reasons for her pre-rehearsal work on the Rodgers and Hammerstein score. Mary McDonnell says pre-rehearsal work "depends on the role," but if there's vocal work to be done, she starts working with a dialect coach. She also "likes to understand a person's time period," so she studies the character from that aspect. Like Joanne Woodward, Mary Alice works out a complete biography of every character she plays, "creating from the play but adding things that are not given in the script." She also finds her character's "secret," because "it gives you a rich inner life." She learned this technique from Lloyd Richards when she first studied acting at the Negro Ensemble Company.

All eight actresses describe, each in her own particular way, that the rehearsal process is finding who the character is and her relation to the other characters. Since she has already felt "a visceral connection" to the character, Cherry Jones likes to use rehearsal clothes very early on in the process, as does Gwen Verdon, who describes in several different situations how rehearsal clothes helped form the characters—notably the "'Erbie Fitch's Twitch" number in *Redhead* and the costume for Charity in *Sweet Charity*. Being what she describes as a "physical" actress, Judith Ivey will use a gesture or "some piece of behavior" as a means of finding the "emotional journey of the character." In this she is like Mary McDonnell, who is constantly searching for "the overall journey of the character." Donna Murphy uses the rehearsal process to make choices about the character. Her discussion of the choices she made for Mrs. Anna in *The King and I* is an important study in understanding how many possibilities are inherent in any well-written character. Sarah Jessica Parker, who loves "flexibility and freedom" as she works, likes a working situation close to the one she had as she rehearsed *Sylvia* where "there were no rules in that room." For Joanne Woodward, the rehearsal process is where she gathers the details that form "the image of the character" she's creating.

All eight actresses are looking for a "connection" between the other characters and their own, and see the other actors as the means of obtaining it. Sarah Jessica Parker wants "collaboration and not locking things in too quickly." For Mary McDonnell, other actors "are like a banquet. I can't wait to be affected by them and to feel what they're going to make me feel." Joanne Woodward believes other actors are so important that you can "play"—an important part of her technique—if they "are on the same wavelength." Ms. Woodward gives fine evidence for this as she discusses the rehearsal situation for the filming of *Mr. and Mrs. Bridge*. Gwen Verdon loves the energy she gets from other performers on stage. "Chita has such energy," she says. "She knows if you're still working on a role. She can see little differences, and she goes right with it. . . . I mean she can critique you and work at the same time."

Costumes are a crucial aspect of understanding and playing a character. Mary McDonnell says, "If I don't have the right costume, I can't do it emotionally." It's as simple as that. Both Cherry Jones and Sarah Jessica Parker are in agreement with her. Ms. Jones says she is "tremendously affected by the costumes" she wears because they're the "external aspect of who you are." Ms. Parker feels costumes are the "exterior that complete the interior life you've been building." She describes with charming grace why she didn't like her costume for *The Substance of Fire* and, more important, why she was wrong. A most surprising discussion is in Gwen Verdon's interview where she tells, with remarkable detail forty years after the fact, how the costume for Anna in *New Girl in Town* was pieced together by herself and designer Rouben Ter-Arutunian. Mary McDonnell describes, with humorous candor, what she learned about herself and the character of Alma Winemiller as she struggled with a costume in *Summer and Smoke*.

Though the main concern of this book is acting for the stage, there are some very astute, and quite important, comments made by these eight women about acting in film and television. Judith Ivey explains that she doesn't approach a character any differently whether it's for stage or film. Neither does Mary Alice, who completes a full biography for every character "whatever the medium," but also says that the "experience creating a character" for film and television "is very different because it's so technical." The discussion of what she learned about film acting while making the film *Sparkle* is a beginning text in film acting technique. Sarah Jessica Parker describes how important it is to "take things down" for film. "Nuances are different on stage than they are on screen," she says. "On screen you can be so little and the camera catches everything. With theatre, the subtleties are bigger. Subtleties on stage would be like fireworks going off in a film." Mary McDonnell says, "I can't be as mysterious" when making a film. The choices have to be more conscious and made more quickly because "there's usually less rehearsal." Joanne Woodward, who has had a most illustrious film career spanning four and a half decades, says, interestingly, that "acting in front of a camera is purgatory. To do it, I have to put myself in a kind of trance." Acting in film, she explains, "has to do with an intense concentration. Ninety percent is concentration, and the only way for me to do that is to stay by myself."

The knowledge in these interviews is formidable, like the eight women who express it. Every anecdote, every detail, every humorous or difficult situation related here—while being specifically about one career and one woman's perception—also serve as a valuable lesson in acting technique. It moves me profoundly that what I began to love so much nearly forty years ago in a darkened movie theatre and that has continued to be a large part of my life can also be a great source of knowledge.